More Book Folding for Beginners

20 Pattern Pack

Folded Book Art Gifts to Make for Free

Holly DiBella-McCarthy

This book is printed in black and white intentionally to allow for more quality beginner friendly patterns at minimal cost. To view completed folded books in color visit:

www.mychicart.com

More Book Folding for Beginners 20 Pattern Pack:
Folded Book Art Gifts to Make for Free

Contact:

mychicart@gmail.com

Credits:
Book Cover Design: Joe McCarthy, neckahneck@gmail.com

Photographs: Author

ISBN: 9798510244670

Printed in the United States of America

A Note from the Author

Free you ask? If you have a Hardcover Book, a pencil, and a ruler, you can make Folded Book Art gifts for free with the Patterns and Instructions in this Book!

More Book Folding for Beginners 20 Pattern Pack follows the 2020 edition of ***Book Folding for Beginners: Step-by-Step Instructions and Patterns***. This book offers new Beginner Friendly Patterns and can be used in addition to the first book, or as an initial introduction to folded book art. A Bonus Open-Heart Pattern for First-Timer success is included. Complete the 101-fold heart pattern in just 2-3 hours!

Folding book art instructions are written for first learners who wish to master this art form. And book folders of all ability levels will achieve professionally folded book results with the included Measure, Mark & Fold Patterns.

This Pattern Pack includes 16 NEW patterns and 4 old favorites. A Book Selection Guide will aid in matching an appropriate book to each Pattern selected.

Want to Learn? Easy How to Fold Books Beginner Friendly Instructions with illustrations; 20 Patterns to choose from requiring just 2 folds per page.

Already Know? Create Professional Folded Books for Gifting, Selling, and Displaying Unique Repurposed Book Art.

Required Supplies: Hardcover Book, Ruler, Folding Tool, Pencil, and a great Pattern.

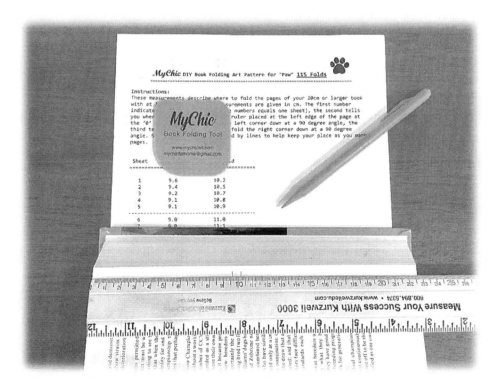

Heartfelt Thanks to my Customers, Followers and Supporters

What an interesting ride moving from a career in education to creating my book art business- MyChicArt. It has been an adventure worth my time as I can continue to teach others, and teaching is what fuels me. Still, I have yet to reach my destination. There are many scenic routes waiting to be explored and countless roads left to discover.

My children inspire me to continue my journey.

Thank You Joseph, Brendan, and Mikayla

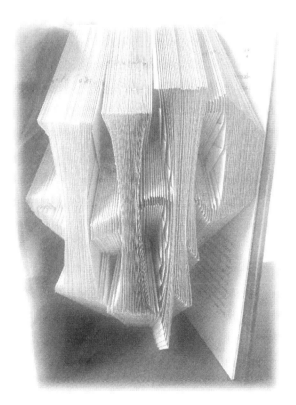

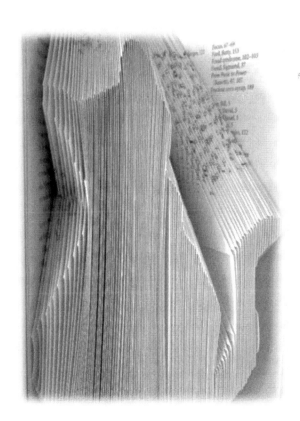

Table of Contents

Spring and Summer Patterns

Fall and Winter Patterns

Fun and Fancy Patterns

Let's Get Started!

*Customer Favorite Patterns from **Book Folding for Beginners: Step-by-Step Instructions & Patterns**, DiBella-McCarthy, 2020

BOOK SELECTION GUIDE

PATTERN	MINIMUM BOOK LENGTH (in cm) RECCOMMENDED	MINIMUM BOOK PAGES REQUIRED	NUMBER OF FOLDS in Pattern
Learning Heart- More fancy than the traditional Learning heart pattern	20	202	101
Let's Go Fly A KITE	24	386	193
Heart Basket	23	344	172
Easter Egg	20	290	145
MoM	20	372	186
#1 Dad	20	496	248
Cross	18	204	102
Hopping Down the BUNNY Trail	22	218	109
Harvest Pumpkin	22	452	226
Football	20	300	150
Double Heart	20	416	208
Christmas Tree	20	314	157
Angel	22	340	170
Snowman	20	278	139
Happy Elephant	23	334	167
Harry Potter Lightening	22	422	211
Cat Woman	20	380	190
Anchor Away	22	328	164
Cat Turned Back	20	274	137
Paw	20	230	115
Butterfly	20	324	162

Instructions

Step 1 – Gather Supplies

Setting up a book folding station with the required supplies on a table or desk will provide you a positive start. Add a comfortable chair and know you can take a break at any point while book marking or folding; simply note your next beginning spot and return when you choose.

A Hardcover Book
Book Dust Jacket
Pattern
Folding Tool
Ruler with metric measurements
Pencil
Scissors*

Hardcover Book

Choose a gently read book in like new or very good condition. The book should be clean, and binding should be straight and tight. Each pattern specifies the recommended book size (by measuring a page top to bottom with a metric ruler.) Each pattern also provides the required number of pages needed to complete the design. You may choose a book that is a longer size or one with more pages than recommended. Since the dust jacket is typically removed to display the completed folded book, be sure to select a cover with a color and title you like. Choosing a cover that matches your fold helps you to connect with your art and personalize to taste. A pink or red cover with the word 'love' in the title is perfect for folding a heart into! Many of the photo illustrations in this Guide show the book *Marley and Me* which was a perfect Title for my Paw of course!

Dust Jacket (or book cover)

The book you choose doesn't absolutely need to have a dust cover. A book dust jacket is listed because it comes in handy holding additional pages back during the marking and folding steps. If your chosen book does not have one you can borrow a book cover from another book on your shelf.

Pattern

The Patterns included in this Beginner's Guide use a Measure, Mark & Fold technique. Patterns are original MyChicArt designs developed for first time folders to use while learning this craft. Of course, book folders of any experience will also enjoy these designs as they showcase well and are faster folds than any of the 'cut and fold' or 'combination' techniques. Most patterns require no cutting when used with the book size specified in the pattern. A few of the designs do require cutting down page length to achieve a professional outcome.

Folding Tool

Beginner book folders may choose to use their finger or an old plastic credit card to crease folds. The *MyChicArt* Folding Tool shown in many of the illustrations works best for this author and is available for purchase at www.mychicart.com

Ruler

The Patterns included in this Guide specify measurements in centimeters (cm) and millimeters (mm) requiring a metric ruler. Most 12-inch rulers display cm/mm measurement marks opposite the inch side.

Pencil

Choose your pencil according to preference. #2 pencils must have a sharp point. Using this type will require a pencil sharpener to keep it sharp throughout the marking process. Mechanical pencils work great and will not require on-going sharpening.

*Scissors

Many of the patterns included in this book will not require scissors when following the book size recommendations. Scissors may be needed with patterns where both marks on the same sheet of paper are exceptionally low or very high on the page.

In this case, you will need to trim the page, so folds lie flat and do not extend beyond the spine. These cuts will <u>not</u> affect the look of your completed design.

Find these 4 Favorite Folds included in this Book from
Book Folding for Beginners: Instructions and Patterns, 2020

Step 2 – Calculate Your Starting Page

Single 'Sheets' of paper in a hardcover book are 'Measured, Marked & Folded' according to a Pattern to create Folded Book Art! Each 'sheet' in a book has 2-page numbers-one on the front, and one on the back of the sheet. Some 'sheets' are unnumbered such as the title page, index, photo pages, etc. The Patterns included in this book provide the sheet number to measure beginning at your calculated starting page number, and the left and right metric measurements to mark on each sheet.

Find your starting page (to center your design in book) using this formula. Example calculation for a pattern requiring **99 Folds** or 'sheets' of paper:

Book Folding Calculation Worksheet		Example	Your Calculation
The last even numbered <u>page</u> in your book		320	
Divide by 2 to get the total foldable **sheets** of paper in your chosen book	/2	160	
Subtract **Folds** required indicated at top of every Pattern	-	99	
Your *starting page number *This number is typically an odd number; if it's an even number simply add 1 and this will be the first page you mark.		61	
NOTES:			

You may have extra unnumbered pages in the front, back, or middle (photo pages for example) of your book. If you want your design exactly centered adjust the starting page accordingly. If for example there are 10 unnumbered pages in the front of the book (5 sheets) and only 2 unnumbered pages (1 sheet) at the end on the book, move your start page back by half the extra sheets. In this example, moving your starting page 2 sheets towards front of the book (page number 57) will result in equal sheets in the front and the back.

You may prefer your folded art is not centered. This is a fine alternative and designs look lovely starting on sheet one or ending on the last sheet of the book. Simply adjust the start page by counting out the number of folds indicated on the pattern.

Photo pages and illustration pages that bleed to page edge of sheet are typically a different color and will show in your folded design. Some folders love the variation, and other folders remove the pages before marking and folding.

Finding your Start Page and Positioning the Book Correctly

Place the book with dust cover on table as if you about to read it.

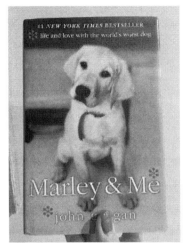

Pick up the book and turn it counterclockwise to your left so spine is in front of you.

This is the position to keep the book facing throughout the measuring/marking/folding process.

Next, Open book to the starting page you calculated on the Book Folding Calculation Worksheet. The sheet to begin marking is furthest from your body. The extra pages can be tucked under the Dust Jacket while you measure, mark and fold to prevent page damage.

Step 3 - Mark Pages

Follow the pattern marking all pages in order. MyChicArt pattern folding numbers are listed in groups of 5 separated by a line. Lines after each set of 5 are simply added to help keep your place.

Go to the starting page number calculated in the Book Folding Calculation Worksheet. Take your metric ruler. Line zero up with the left corner of your page. Leave a bit of space to make marks; do not mark right on the page edge. Without moving the ruler, place your 2 marks with a sharp pencil on the two measurements the pattern indicates. In this example the measurements on the pattern for sheet 1 are 9.6 and 10.2- Make these two marks on your first sheet.

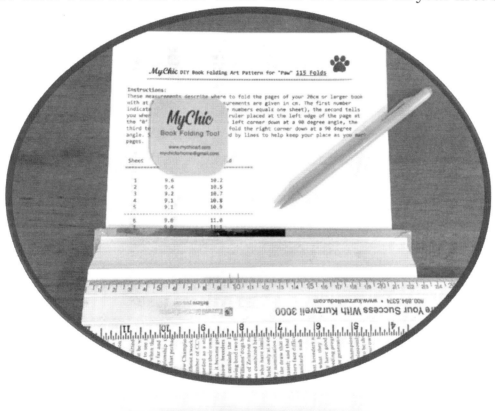

Next, turn the page to measure and mark sheet 2. Read the pattern to see where to place the two marks on that page. Continue to follow the pattern to the end until all sheets are marked.

Step 4: Fold Pages

Fold each sheet in order exactly on the two marks (Left corner down; right corner down.) Try to keep the folds at an angle of 90 degrees, or as closely as you can. Now press your finger down to crease on the mark starting at the page edge and slide your finger down the fold.

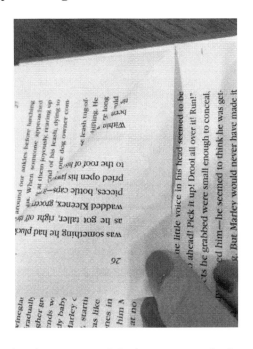 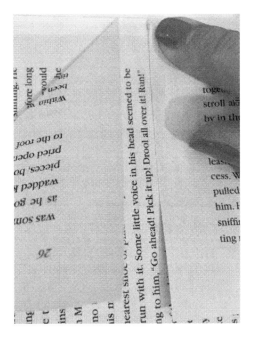

Fold each sheet at a 90-degree angle by starting the crease at your mark and lining the fold up with a line of print. A professionally finished design will result when all sheets in the pattern are folded at 90 degrees.

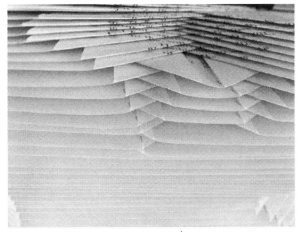

Use your fingernail, old credit card or MyChicArt Folding Tool to create a crisp crease on each fold before moving on to fold the next sheet. For professional results, do not skip this step!

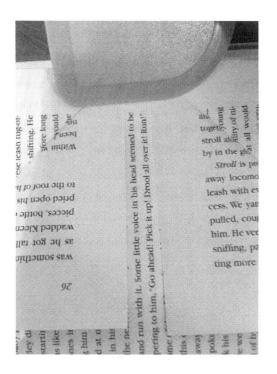
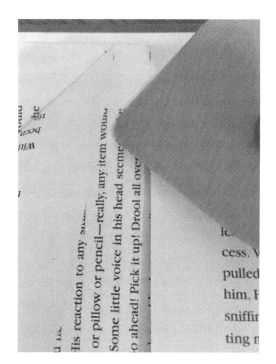

When left or right folded paper is too long to lay flat because it extends beyond the book spine, simply trim the excess in a straight line with scissors. Many patterns included in *More Book Folding for Beginners* will not require page trimming, and this will only be necessary if you chose a book shorter than the size recommended in the pattern. The Patterns in this edition which *may* require some page trimming include Kite, Pumpkin, Football, Tree, Elephant, HP, Anchor and Butterfly. For example, the first 6 folds in the Butterfly pattern require approximately 2cm be trimmed from the right-side fold allow the paper to lie flat. The amount trimmed can be wider than is necessary to avoid the fold extending beyond the book spine. The width you choose to trim will not affect the look of the completed book.

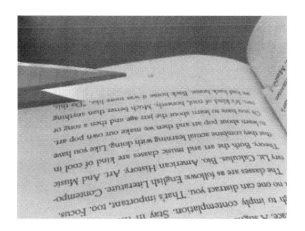
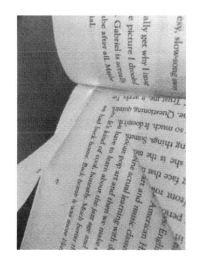

Step 5: Finishing Tips   Celebrate your Folded Book Art!

If your pattern spreads out more than you prefer, you may choose to 'flatten' the pattern for several hours by stacking books on top or by putting a rubber band around the closed book. If you notice a mistake, check the pattern and re-mark-re-fold the affected sheet.

Remove the Dust Jacket. Embellish with ribbon or twine if you choose and Display!

Ribbon can be attached using double sided tape. Place the tape on the end of one side of the ribbon. Wrap the ribbon around extra pages and secure the opposite edge over the tape for a tight fit. The taped part can be hidden by moving it behind your first fold. Twine, yarn or rope can also be tied on vertically or horizontally. You may prefer to keep the dust cover on if meaningful. Harry Potter Fans will want you to leave the cover on!

Patterns

Recommended First Pattern! This Bonus Pattern is included for first time folders. The Open-Heart pattern has been designed to produce fast-start success; and to engage, excite, and motivate book folders to try the next pattern in this book, and the next…

==

Best 'First Time Folder' Pattern Anywhere!
These measurements describe where to mark and fold the pages of your 20cm or longer book with at least 202-page numbers. All measurements are given in cm. The first number indicates the sheet number (2-page numbers equals one sheet); the second tells you where (measured with a metric ruler placed on the left edge of the page at the '0' mark) to mark and then fold the left corner down at a 90-degree angle; the third number tells you where to mark and then fold the right corner down at a 90-degree angle. Each set of 5 sheets is separated by lines to help keep your place as you mark pages.
Follow Instructions detailed (p. 12-20) to create your first Folded Book!

Sheet	Left Fold	Right Fold
1	8.4	8.5
2	7.3	9.5
3	6.9	9.9
4	6.6	10.3
5	6.3	10.5
6	6.1	10.8
7	5.9	11.0
8	5.7	11.2
9	5.5	11.3
10	5.4	7.7
11	9.6	11.7
12	5.2	7.0
13	10.1	11.9
14	5.0	6.6

15	10.4	12.2

16	4.8	6.3
17	10.8	12.4
18	4.7	6.1
19	11.0	12.6
20	4.6	5.9

21	11.3	12.8
22	4.5	5.8
23	11.5	13.1
24	4.5	5.8
25	11.7	13.3

26	4.5	5.7
27	11.9	13.5
28	4.5	5.8
29	12.1	13.7
30	4.5	5.8

31	12.4	14.0
32	4.5	5.9
33	12.6	14.2
34	4.7	6.0
35	12.8	14.5

36	4.8	6.2
37	13.1	14.8
38	4.9	6.4

39	13.3	15.0
40	5.1	6.7

41	13.6	15.4
42	5.3	7.0
43	13.9	15.7
44	5.5	7.3
45	14.2	16.1

46	5.8	7.7
47	14.5	16.5
48	6.1	8.1
49	14.8	16.9
50	6.4	8.4

51	15.1	17.4
52	6.4	8.4
53	14.8	16.9
54	6.1	8.1
55	14.5	16.5

56	5.8	7.7
57	14.2	16.1
58	5.5	7.3
59	13.9	15.7
60	5.3	7.0

61	13.6	15.4
62	5.1	6.7

63	13.3	15.0
64	4.9	6.4
65	13.1	14.8
----	----	----
66	4.8	6.2
67	12.8	14.5
68	4.7	6.0
69	12.6	14.2
70	4.5	5.9
----	----	----
71	12.4	14.0
72	4.5	5.8
73	12.1	13.7
74	4.5	5.8
75	11.9	13.5
----	----	----
76	4.5	5.7
77	11.7	13.3
78	4.5	5.8
79	11.5	13.1
80	4.5	5.8
----	----	----
81	11.3	12.8
82	4.6	5.9
83	11.0	12.6
84	4.7	6.1
85	10.8	12.4
----	----	----
86	4.8	6.3

87	10.4	12.2
88	5.0	6.6
89	10.1	11.9
90	5.2	7.0

91	9.6	11.7
92	5.4	7.7
93	5.5	11.3
94	5.7	11.2
95	5.9	11.0

96	6.1	10.8
97	6.3	10.5
98	6.6	10.3
99	6.9	9.9
100	7.3	9.5

101	8.4	8.5

Now that you have marked all the Sheets- **HAVE FUN FOLDING!**

==

Let's Go Fly a KITE! These measurements describe where to mark and fold the pages of your 24cm or longer book with at least 386-page numbers. All measurements are given in cm. The first number indicates the sheet number (2-page numbers equals one sheet, the second tells you where (measured with a metric ruler placed at the left edge of the page at the '0' mark) to mark and then fold the left corner down at a 90-degree angle; the third number tells you where to mark and then fold the right corner down at a 90-degree angle.

Sheet	Left Fold	Right Fold
1	19.3	19.5
2	19.3	19.5
3	19.3	19.5
4	19.2	19.5
5	19.2	19.5
6	19.2	19.4
7	19.1	19.4
8	19.1	19.4
9	19.1	19.3
10	19.0	19.3
11	17.2	17.6
12	18.9	19.2
13	17.0	17.6
14	18.8	19.1
15	16.8	17.7
16	18.7	19.1

17	16.6	17.7
18	18.6	18.9
19	16.5	17.8
20	18.5	18.8
---	---	---
21	16.4	17.8
22	18.3	18.7
23	16.7	17.9
24	18.2	18.5
25	17.2	17.9
---	---	---
26	17.4	18.4
27	17.7	18.3
28	17.8	18.3
29	14.4	14.9
30	17.6	18.7
---	---	---
31	14.1	14.9
32	18.0	19.2
33	13.7	14.9
34	17.1	17.6
35	18.1	19.5
---	---	---
36	13.5	14.9
37	16.6	17.2
38	18.2	19.3
39	13.9	14.9
40	16.0	16.7
---	---	---
41	18.3	19.0
42	14.2	14.9

43	15.2	16.0
44	18.3	18.7
45	14.6	15.5

46	18.5	18.5
47	14.5	15.1
48	14.3	15.1
49	14.2	14.7
50	14.8	15.4

51	14.0	14.4
52	14.8	15.6
53	13.8	14.2
54	14.8	15.8
55	13.7	14.0

56	14.8	16.1
57	11.5	11.8
58	13.4	13.8
59	14.8	16.1
60	11.3	11.9

61	13.2	13.5
62	14.8	15.6
63	11.1	12.1
64	13.0	13.3
65	14.8	15.1

66	12.8	13.2
67	10.9	12.3
68	12.7	13.0

69	10.8	12.4
70	12.6	12.9

71	10.8	12.5
72	11.2	12.8
73	11.7	12.8
74	12.2	12.9
75	12.3	13.4

76	12.3	13.9
77	12.2	12.6
78	12.7	14.3
79	12.1	12.4
80	12.7	14.2

81	12.0	12.3
82	12.8	14.1
83	11.9	12.2
84	12.9	13.9
85	11.7	12.1

86	13.0	13.8
87	11.6	11.9
88	13.1	13.7
89	11.5	11.8
90	13.2	13.6

91	11.3	11.7
92	11.3	11.6
93	10.9	11.0
94	10.5	11.0

95	10.2	10.9

96	9.9	10.8
97	9.6	10.7
98	11.2	11.4
99	9.0	10.5
100	11.0	11.3

101	8.4	10.4
102	10.8	11.3
103	7.7	10.2
104	10.7	11.2
105	7.1	10.0

106	10.5	11.2
107	6.5	9.8
108	10.3	11.1
109	5.8	9.7
110	10.1	11.1

111	5.2	9.5
112	10.0	11.0
113	4.5	9.3
114	9.8	11.0
115	3.9	9.1

116	9.6	10.9
117	3.3	8.9
118	9.4	10.9
119	2.7	8.8
120	9.3	10.8

121	2.8	8.6
122	9.1	10.8
123	3.0	8.4
124	3.1	8.3
125	8.8	10.7
126	2.5	2.7
127	3.4	8.1
128	8.5	10.6
129	2.5	3.0
130	3.6	7.8
131	8.3	10.5
132	2.5	3.2
133	3.9	7.5
134	8.0	10.5
135	2.5	3.5
136	4.2	7.3
137	7.8	10.4
138	2.5	3.8
139	4.4	7.0
140	7.5	10.3
141	2.5	4.0
142	4.7	6.7
143	7.2	10.3
144	2.5	4.3
145	5.0	6.5

146	7.0	10.2
147	2.5	4.6
148	5.2	6.2
149	6.7	10.1
150	2.5	4.8
151	5.5	5.9
152	6.4	10.0
153	2.5	5.1
154	6.2	10.0
155	2.5	5.3
156	6.1	9.9
157	2.5	5.4
158	6.1	9.9
159	2.5	5.2
160	6.3	9.8
161	6.4	9.8
162	2.5	5.0
163	5.5	6.0
164	6.6	9.7
165	2.5	4.7
166	5.2	6.2
167	6.9	9.6
168	2.5	4.4
169	4.9	6.5
170	7.2	9.6
171	2.5	4.2

172	4.7	6.8
173	7.4	9.5
174	2.5	3.9
175	4.4	7.0
- -		
176	7.7	9.4
177	2.5	3.6
178	4.1	7.3
179	8.0	9.3
180	2.5	3.4
- -		
181	3.9	7.6
182	8.2	9.3
183	2.5	3.1
184	3.6	7.8
185	8.5	9.2
- -		
186	2.5	2.9
187	3.3	8.1
188	8.8	9.1
189	2.5	2.6
190	8.9	9.1
- -		
191	3.0	8.4
192	2.9	8.5
193	2.8	8.6

Remember! When left or right folded paper is too long to lay flat because it extends beyond the book spine use scissors. Simply trim the excess in a straight line from page edge toward book spine and gently tear off the excess. The amount trimmed can be wider than is necessary to prevent the fold extending beyond the book spine. The width you choose to trim will not affect the look of the completed book.

==

These measurements describe where to mark and fold the pages of your 23cm or longer book with at least 344-page numbers. All measurements are given in cm. The first number indicates the sheet number (2-page numbers equals one sheet); the second tells you where (measured with a metric ruler placed at the left edge of the page at the '0' mark) to mark and then fold the left corner down at a 90-degree angle; the third number tells you where to mark and then fold the right corner down at a 90-degree angle.

Sheet	Left Fold	Right Fold
1	10.8	11.3
2	10.7	11.6
3	10.6	11.8
4	10.5	12.1
5	10.5	12.4
6	10.4	12.7
7	10.4	12.9
8	10.4	13.2
9	10.4	13.5
10	10.4	13.8
11	10.4	14.1
12	10.4	14.3
13	10.1	14.6
14	9.6	14.9
15	9.2	15.2
16	8.8	15.5
17	8.6	15.8
18	8.3	16.0

19	8.1	16.3
20	7.9	16.6
------	------	------
21	7.7	16.8
22	7.6	16.9
23	7.4	17.1
24	7.3	9.8
25	10.4	17.2
------	------	------
26	7.0	9.1
27	10.4	17.3
28	6.7	8.6
29	10.4	17.4
30	6.5	8.2
------	------	------
31	10.4	17.5
32	6.3	7.8
33	10.4	17.5
34	6.0	7.5
35	10.4	17.6
------	------	------
36	5.9	7.3
37	10.4	17.6
38	5.7	7.0
39	10.4	17.6
40	5.5	6.8
------	------	------
41	10.4	17.6
42	5.4	6.6
43	10.4	17.6
44	5.2	6.5

45	10.4	17.6

46	5.1	6.3
47	10.4	17.6
48	5.0	6.1
49	10.4	17.6
50	4.9	6.0

51	10.4	17.6
52	4.8	5.8
53	10.4	17.6
54	4.7	5.7
55	10.4	17.6

56	4.6	5.6
57	10.4	17.6
58	4.5	5.5
59	10.4	17.6
60	4.4	5.4

61	10.4	17.6
62	4.7	5.3
63	10.4	17.6
64	4.9	5.3
65	3.6	4.3

66	3.4	4.6
67	10.4	17.6
68	3.2	4.9
69	10.4	17.6
70	3.1	5.1

71	10.4	17.6
72	3.0	5.3
73	10.4	17.6
74	3.0	5.4
75	10.4	17.6
---	---	---
76	3.0	5.6
77	10.4	17.6
78	3.1	5.7
79	10.4	17.6
80	3.1	5.8
---	---	---
81	10.4	17.6
82	3.2	5.9
83	10.4	17.6
84	3.3	6.0
85	10.4	17.6
---	---	---
86	3.5	6.0
87	10.4	17.6
88	3.4	6.0
89	10.4	17.6
90	3.3	5.9
---	---	---
91	10.4	17.6
92	3.2	5.8
93	10.4	17.6
94	3.1	5.7
95	10.4	17.6
---	---	---
96	3.0	5.6

97	10.4	17.6
98	3.0	5.5
99	10.4	17.6
100	3.0	5.4
101	10.4	17.6
102	3.1	5.2
103	10.4	17.6
104	3.2	5.0
105	10.4	17.6
106	3.3	4.8
107	10.4	17.6
108	10.4	17.6
109	3.6	4.4
110	4.9	5.3
111	10.4	17.6
112	4.5	5.3
113	10.4	17.6
114	4.3	5.4
115	10.4	17.6
116	4.4	5.5
117	10.4	17.6
118	4.5	5.6
119	10.4	17.6
120	4.6	5.7
121	10.4	17.6
122	4.7	5.8

123	10.4	17.6
124	4.8	6.0
125	10.4	17.6
--		
126	4.9	6.1
127	10.4	17.6
128	5.0	6.3
129	10.4	17.6
130	5.1	6.5
--		
131	10.4	17.6
132	5.2	6.6
133	10.4	17.6
134	5.4	6.8
135	10.4	17.6
--		
136	5.5	7.0
137	10.4	17.6
138	5.7	7.3
139	10.4	17.5
140	5.9	7.6
--		
141	10.4	17.5
142	6.1	7.9
143	10.4	17.4
144	6.3	8.2
145	10.4	17.3
--		
146	6.5	8.6
147	10.4	17.2
148	6.7	9.1

149	10.4	17.0
150	7.0	9.8

151	7.1	16.7
152	7.3	16.5
153	7.4	16.2
154	7.6	16.0
155	7.8	15.7

156	7.9	15.4
157	8.2	15.2
158	8.4	14.9
159	8.6	14.7
160	8.9	14.4

161	9.2	14.1
162	9.6	13.9
163	10.2	13.6
164	10.4	13.3
165	10.4	13.1

166	10.4	12.8
167	10.4	12.6
168	10.4	12.3
169	10.5	12.1
170	10.6	11.8

171	10.6	11.6
172	10.8	11.3

==

Instructions:

These measurements describe where to mark and fold the pages of your 20cm or longer book with at least 290-page numbers. All measurements are given in cm. The first number indicates the sheet number (2-page numbers equals one sheet, the second tells you where (measured with a metric ruler placed at the left edge of the page at the '0' mark) to mark and then fold the left corner down at a 90-degree angle; the third number tells you where to mark and then fold the right corner down at a 90-degree angle.

Sheet	Left Fold	Right Fold
1	11.0	11.2
2	12.2	12.9
3	10.1	11.1
4	12.1	13.5
5	9.5	11.0
6	11.9	13.9
7	9.0	10.9
8	11.8	14.3
9	8.6	10.8
10	11.8	14.6
11	8.2	10.8
12	11.9	14.8
13	8.2	10.9
14	12.0	15.1
15	8.3	11.0
16	12.1	15.3

17	12.1	15.4
18	7.0	7.4
19	8.5	11.2
20	12.3	15.7

21	6.5	7.6
22	8.6	11.4
23	12.4	15.9
24	6.1	7.7
25	8.8	11.6

26	12.6	16.1
27	5.7	7.9
28	9.0	11.7
29	12.8	16.3
30	5.4	8.1

31	9.1	11.9
32	12.9	16.5
33	5.0	8.2
34	9.3	12.0
35	13.1	16.6

36	4.7	8.4
37	9.4	12.2
38	13.2	16.8
39	4.4	8.5
40	9.6	12.3

41	13.3	16.9
42	4.1	8.6
43	9.6	12.3
44	13.3	17.0
45	3.8	8.5

46	9.4	12.2
47	13.1	17.1
48	3.6	8.3
49	9.3	12.0
50	13.0	17.2

51	3.4	8.2
52	9.1	11.8
53	12.8	17.3
54	3.2	8.0
55	8.9	11.7

56	12.7	17.3
57	3.0	7.8
58	8.8	11.5
59	12.5	17.4
60	2.8	7.7

61	8.6	11.4
62	12.3	17.4
63	2.7	7.5
64	8.5	11.2
65	12.2	17.4

----	----	----
66	2.6	7.4
67	8.3	11.1
68	12.0	17.5
69	2.5	7.2
70	8.2	10.9
----	----	----
71	11.9	17.5
72	2.5	7.1
73	8.0	10.8
74	11.8	17.5
75	2.5	7.1
----	----	----
76	8.2	10.9
77	12.0	17.5
78	2.5	7.3
79	8.3	11.1
80	12.1	17.5
----	----	----
81	2.6	7.4
82	8.5	11.2
83	12.3	17.4
84	2.7	7.6
85	8.6	11.4
----	----	----
86	12.4	17.4
87	2.9	7.7
88	8.8	11.5
89	12.6	17.3

90	3.0	7.9

91	8.9	11.7
92	12.8	17.3
93	3.2	8.0
94	9.1	11.8
95	12.9	17.2

96	3.4	8.2
97	9.3	12.0
98	13.1	17.1
99	3.7	8.4
100	9.4	12.2

101	13.2	17.0
102	3.9	8.5
103	9.6	12.3
104	13.3	16.9
105	4.2	8.6

106	9.6	12.3
107	13.3	16.8
108	4.5	8.5
109	9.4	12.2
110	13.1	16.7

111	4.8	8.3
112	9.3	12.0
113	13.0	16.5

114	5.1	8.2
115	9.1	11.9

116	12.8	16.4
117	5.5	8.0
118	9.0	11.7
119	12.7	16.2
120	5.9	7.8

121	8.8	11.6
122	12.5	16.0
123	6.3	7.7
124	8.6	11.4
125	12.3	15.7

126	6.7	7.5
127	8.5	11.2
128	12.2	15.5
129	7.2	7.4
130	12.1	15.3

131	8.3	11.0
132	12.0	15.1
133	8.2	10.9
134	11.9	14.8
135	8.2	10.8

136	11.8	14.6
137	8.6	10.8

138	11.8	14.3
139	9.0	10.9
140	11.9	13.9
--		
141	9.5	11.0
142	12.1	13.5
143	10.1	11.1
144	12.2	12.9
145	11.0	11.2

Now that you have marked all the Sheets- **FOLD and Decorate!**

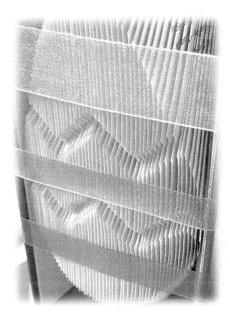

MyChicArt Book Folding Art Pattern for **MOM 186 folds**

==

Instructions:

These measurements describe where to mark and fold the pages of your 20cm or larger book with at least 372 page numbers. All measurements are given in cm. The first number indicates the sheet number (2 page numbers equals one sheet), the second tells you where (measured with a cm ruler placed at the left edge of the page at the '0' mark) to mark and then fold the left corner down at a 90 degree angle, the third number tells you where to mark and then fold the right corner down at a 90 degree angle.

Sheet	Left Fold	Right Fold
1	5.8	12.0
2	5.8	12.1
3	5.8	12.1
4	5.8	12.1
5	5.8	12.1
6	5.8	12.1
7	5.8	12.1
8	5.8	12.1
9	5.8	12.1
10	5.8	12.1
11	5.8	12.1
12	5.8	12.1
13	5.8	12.1
14	5.8	12.1
15	5.8	8.2
16	5.8	8.2

17	5.8	8.7
18	5.8	9.0
19	5.8	9.3
20	5.8	9.5

21	5.8	9.8
22	5.8	10.1
23	6.0	10.4
24	6.3	10.7
25	6.6	11.0

26	6.9	11.3
27	7.2	11.6
28	7.5	11.9
29	7.8	12.1
30	8.1	12.1

31	8.3	12.1
32	8.6	12.1
33	8.9	12.1
34	9.2	12.1
35	9.5	12.1

36	9.7	12.1
37	9.4	12.1
38	9.2	12.1
39	8.9	12.1
40	8.6	12.1

41	8.3	12.1
42	8.0	12.0

43	7.7	11.7
44	7.4	11.4
45	7.1	11.1
---	---	---
46	6.8	10.7
47	6.5	10.5
48	6.2	10.2
49	5.9	9.9
50	5.8	9.6
---	---	---
51	5.8	9.3
52	5.8	9.0
53	5.8	8.7
54	5.8	8.5
55	5.8	8.2
---	---	---
56	5.8	12.0
57	5.8	12.1
58	5.8	12.1
59	5.8	12.1
60	5.8	12.1
---	---	---
61	5.8	12.1
62	5.8	12.1
63	5.8	12.1
64	5.8	12.1
65	5.8	12.1
---	---	---
66	5.8	12.1
67	5.8	12.1
68	5.8	12.1

69	5.8	12.1
70	5.8	12.0

71	7.9	8.9
72	7.6	9.2
73	7.3	9.4
74	7.1	9.5
75	7.0	9.7

76	6.9	9.8
77	6.8	9.9
78	6.7	10.0
79	6.7	10.1
80	6.6	10.2

81	6.6	10.2
82	6.6	10.3
83	6.6	10.4
84	6.6	10.5
85	6.7	10.5

86	6.7	10.6
87	6.7	10.7
88	6.8	10.9
89	6.9	11.0
90	7.0	11.1

91	7.1	11.2
92	7.3	11.4
93	7.5	11.6
94	7.6	11.7

95	7.3	11.5
96	7.2	11.3
97	7.1	11.2
98	7.0	11.1
99	6.9	10.9
100	6.8	10.8
101	6.7	10.7
102	6.7	10.6
103	6.7	10.5
104	6.6	10.4
105	6.6	10.3
106	6.6	10.2
107	6.7	10.2
108	6.7	10.1
109	6.7	10.0
110	6.8	9.9
111	6.9	9.8
112	6.9	9.7
113	7.1	9.6
114	7.2	9.4
115	7.4	9.3
116	7.7	9.0
117	5.8	12.0
118	5.8	12.1
119	5.8	12.1
120	5.8	12.1

```
------------------------------------------------

121          5.8            12.1

122          5.8            12.1

123          5.8            12.1

124          5.8            12.1

125          5.8            12.1

------------------------------------------------

126          5.8            12.1

127          5.8            12.1

128          5.8            12.1

129          5.8            12.1

130          5.8            12.1

------------------------------------------------

131          5.8             8.2

132          5.8             8.2

133          5.8             8.7

134          5.8             9.0

135          5.8             9.3

------------------------------------------------

136          5.8             9.5

137          5.8             9.8

138          5.8            10.1

139          6.0            10.4

140          6.3            10.7

------------------------------------------------

141          6.6            11.0

142          6.9            11.3

143          7.2            11.6

144          7.5            11.9

145          7.8            12.1

------------------------------------------------
```

146	8.1	12.1
147	8.3	12.1
148	8.6	12.1
149	8.9	12.1
150	9.2	12.1
--		
151	9.5	12.1
152	9.7	12.1
153	9.4	12.1
154	9.2	12.1
155	8.9	12.1
--		
156	8.6	12.1
157	8.3	12.1
158	8.0	12.0
159	7.7	11.7
160	7.4	11.4
--		
161	7.1	11.1
162	6.8	10.7
163	6.5	10.5
164	6.2	10.2
165	5.9	9.9
--		
166	5.8	9.6
167	5.8	9.3
168	5.8	9.0
169	5.8	8.7
170	5.8	8.5
--		
171	5.8	8.2

172	5.8	12.0
173	5.8	12.1
174	5.8	12.1
175	5.8	12.1
------	------	------
176	5.8	12.1
177	5.8	12.1
178	5.8	12.1
179	5.8	12.1
180	5.8	12.1
------	------	------
181	5.8	12.1
182	5.8	12.1
183	5.8	12.1
184	5.8	12.1
185	5.8	12.1
186	5.8	12.0

Now that you finished marking- FOLD A Favorite Mom a Beautiful Keepsake!

==

Instructions:

These measurements describe where to mark and fold the pages of your 20 cm or longer book with at least 496-page numbers. All measurements are given in cm. The first number indicates the sheet number (2-page numbers equals one sheet), the second tells you where (measured with a cm ruler placed at the left edge of the page at the '0' mark) to mark and then fold the left corner down at a 90-degree angle; the third number tells you where to mark and then fold the right corner down at a 90-degree angle.

Sheet	Left Fold	Right Fold
1	11.7	11.8
2	11.2	11.8
3	11.2	11.8
4	9.2	9.5
5	11.2	11.8
6	8.9	9.5
7	11.2	11.8
8	8.9	9.5
9	11.2	11.8
10	8.9	9.5
11	11.2	11.8
12	12.9	13.4
13	8.9	9.5
14	11.2	13.4
15	8.9	9.5
16	10.3	13.4
17	8.9	13.4
18	8.8	12.8
19	8.1	12.1

20	7.8	11.8
---	---	---
21	7.2	11.1
22	11.2	11.8
23	7.2	10.2
24	11.2	11.8
25	7.2	9.5
---	---	---
26	11.2	11.8
27	7.2	8.0
28	8.9	9.5
29	11.2	11.8
30	8.9	9.5
---	---	---
31	11.2	11.8
32	8.9	9.5
33	11.2	11.8
34	8.9	9.5
35	11.2	11.8
---	---	---
36	13.1	13.4
37	8.9	9.5
38	11.2	13.4
39	8.9	9.5
40	10.5	13.4
---	---	---
41	8.9	9.5
42	9.6	13.4
43	8.6	12.6
44	8.0	12.0
45	7.3	11.8

46	7.2	11.0
47	11.2	11.8
48	7.2	9.7
49	11.2	11.8
50	7.2	8.8

51	8.9	9.5
52	11.2	11.8
53	8.9	9.5
54	11.2	11.8
55	8.9	9.5

56	11.2	11.8
57	8.9	9.5
58	11.2	11.8
59	8.9	9.5
60	8.9	9.5

61	8.9	9.3
62	7.3	7.4
63	7.3	7.9
64	7.2	8.0
65	13.2	14.3

66	7.1	8.0
67	13.2	14.3
68	7.0	7.9
69	13.2	14.3
70	6.9	7.9

71	13.2	14.3

72	6.8	7.9
73	13.2	14.3
74	6.7	7.8
75	13.2	14.3

76	6.6	7.8
77	13.2	14.3
78	6.5	7.7
79	13.2	14.3
80	6.5	7.7

81	13.2	14.3
82	6.4	14.3
83	6.3	14.3
84	6.2	14.3
85	6.2	14.3

86	6.2	14.3
87	6.1	14.3
88	6.1	14.3
89	6.0	14.3
90	6.0	14.3

91	5.9	14.3
92	5.9	14.3
93	5.8	14.3
94	5.8	14.3
95	13.2	14.3

96	13.2	14.3
97	13.2	14.3

98	13.2	14.3
99	13.2	14.3
100	13.2	14.3
-------	-------	-------
101	13.2	14.3
102	13.2	14.3
103	13.2	14.3
104	13.2	14.3
105	6.9	13.0
-------	-------	-------
106	6.8	13.1
107	6.8	13.1
108	6.8	13.1
109	6.8	13.1
110	6.8	13.1
-------	-------	-------
111	6.8	13.1
112	6.8	13.1
113	6.8	13.1
114	6.8	13.1
115	6.8	13.1
-------	-------	-------
116	6.8	13.1
117	6.8	13.1
118	6.8	13.1
119	6.8	13.1
120	6.8	13.1
-------	-------	-------
121	6.8	8.1
122	11.7	13.1
123	6.8	8.1

124	11.7	13.1
125	6.8	8.1

126	11.7	13.1
127	6.8	8.1
128	11.7	13.1
129	6.8	8.1
130	11.7	13.1

131	6.8	8.2
132	11.6	13.0
133	6.8	8.2
134	11.6	13.0
135	6.8	8.3

136	11.5	13.0
137	6.9	8.5
138	11.3	12.9
139	6.9	8.6
140	11.1	12.9

141	7.0	8.9
142	10.9	12.8
143	7.0	12.7
144	7.1	12.7
145	7.1	12.6

146	7.2	12.6
147	7.2	12.5
148	7.3	12.4
149	7.4	12.3

150	7.4	12.2
151	7.5	12.1
152	7.6	12.0
153	7.7	11.9
154	7.8	11.8
155	8.0	11.6
156	8.2	11.4
157	8.4	11.2
158	8.7	10.9
159	9.1	10.5
160	11.4	12.0
161	11.1	12.4
162	10.9	12.6
163	10.7	12.7
164	10.6	12.8
165	8.8	10.0
166	10.5	12.9
167	8.7	9.9
168	10.4	13.0
169	8.6	9.8
170	10.3	13.1
171	8.5	9.7
172	10.3	13.1
173	8.5	9.7
174	10.2	13.2
175	8.4	9.6

```
-------------------------------------------------

176        10.2              11.3

177        11.8              13.2

178         8.4               9.6

179        10.1              11.2

180        12.0              13.1

-------------------------------------------------

181         8.4               9.6

182        10.1              11.1

183        12.0              13.0

184         8.4               9.7

185        10.1              11.1

-------------------------------------------------

186        11.8              12.9

187         8.4              13.1

188         8.5              13.1

189         8.5              13.1

190         8.5              13.1

-------------------------------------------------

191         8.6              13.1

192         8.6              13.1

193         8.6              13.1

194         8.7              13.1

195         8.8              13.1

-------------------------------------------------

196         8.9              13.1

197         9.0              13.1

198         9.1              13.1

199         9.3              13.1

200         9.6              13.0

201        11.4              11.5 (fold point back toward spine)
```

202	10.6	11.1
203	10.0	11.8
204	9.7	12.0
205	9.5	12.2
206	9.3	12.4
207	9.2	12.5
208	9.0	12.7
209	8.9	12.8
210	8.8	12.8
211	8.8	12.9
212	8.7	12.9
213	8.6	13.0
214	8.6	13.0
215	8.5	13.1
216	8.5	13.1
217	8.5	13.1
218	8.4	10.7
219	11.0	13.1
220	8.4	10.0
221	11.7	13.2
222	8.4	9.8
223	11.8	13.2
224	8.4	9.7
225	11.9	13.1
226	8.4	9.7
227	11.9	13.1

228	8.5	9.7
229	11.9	13.0
230	8.5	9.8

231	11.7	12.9
232	8.7	10.0
233	11.5	12.8
234	6.4	13.0
235	6.4	13.1

236	6.4	13.1
237	6.4	13.1
238	6.4	13.1
239	6.4	13.1
240	6.4	13.1

241	6.4	13.1
242	6.4	13.1
243	6.4	13.1
244	6.4	13.1
245	6.4	13.1

246	6.4	13.1
247	6.4	13.1
248	6.4	13.0 Pattern copyright of *MyChicArt*

==

Instructions:
These measurements describe where to fold the pages of your 18cm or larger book with at least 204 page numbers. All measurements are given in cm. The first number indicates the sheet number (2 page numbers equals one sheet), the second tells you where (measured with a cm ruler placed at the left edge of the page at the '0' mark) to mark and fold the left corner down at a 90 degree angle, the third tells you where to mark and fold the right corner down at a 90 degree angle.

Sheet	Left Fold	Right Fold
1	8.3	10.8
2	8.2	11.0
3	8.1	11.0
4	8.1	11.0
5	8.1	11.1
6	8.1	11.1
7	8.1	11.0
8	8.2	11.0
9	8.2	11.0
10	8.2	10.9
11	8.2	10.9
12	8.3	10.8
13	8.3	10.8
14	8.3	10.8
15	8.4	10.8

16	8.4	10.7
17	8.4	10.7
18	8.4	10.7
19	8.4	10.7
20	8.4	10.7
----	----	----
21	8.5	10.7
22	8.5	10.7
23	8.5	10.7
24	8.4	10.7
25	8.4	10.7
----	----	----
26	8.4	10.7
27	8.4	10.7
28	8.4	10.7
29	8.4	10.7
30	8.3	10.8
----	----	----
31	14.5	15.4
32	8.2	10.9
33	13.8	15.7
34	8.0	11.1
35	13.0	15.7
----	----	----
36	5.9	15.7
37	5.8	15.7
38	5.7	15.7
39	5.7	15.7
40	5.7	15.7
----	----	----
41	5.7	15.7

42	5.7	15.7
43	5.7	15.7
44	5.7	15.7
45	5.7	15.7

46	5.7	15.7
47	5.7	15.7
48	5.6	15.7
49	5.6	15.7
50	5.6	15.7

51	5.6	15.7
52	5.6	15.7
53	5.6	15.7
54	5.6	15.7
55	5.6	15.7

56	5.7	15.7
57	5.7	15.7
58	5.7	15.7
59	5.7	15.7
60	5.7	15.7

61	5.7	15.7
62	5.7	15.7
63	5.7	15.7
64	5.7	15.7
65	5.8	15.7

66	5.9	15.7
67	5.9	15.7

68	13.0	15.7
69	8.0	11.1
70	13.8	15.7
----	----	----
71	8.2	10.9
72	14.5	15.4
73	8.3	10.8
74	8.4	10.7
75	8.4	10.7
----	----	----
76	8.4	10.7
77	8.4	10.7
78	8.4	10.7
79	8.4	10.7
80	8.5	10.7

81	8.5	10.7
82	8.5	10.7
83	8.4	10.7
84	8.4	10.7
85	8.4	10.7
---	---	---
86	8.4	10.7
87	8.4	10.7
88	8.4	10.8
89	8.3	10.8
90	8.3	10.8
---	---	---
91	8.3	10.8
92	8.2	10.9
93	8.2	10.9
94	8.2	11.0
95	8.2	11.0
---	---	---
96	8.1	11.0
97	8.1	11.1
98	8.1	11.1
99	8.1	11.0
100	8.1	11.0
---	---	---
101	8.2	11.0
102	8.3	10.8

Now that you have marked all the Sheets- **FOLD for a friend's bookshelf!**

MyChicArt Book Folding Pattern for **Bunny 109 Folds**
===

Instructions:
These measurements describe where to mark and fold the pages of your 22cm or larger book with at least 218-page numbers. All measurements are given in cm. The first number indicates the sheet number (2-page numbers equals one sheet), the second tells you where (measured with a cm ruler placed at the left edge of the page at the '0' mark) to mark and then fold the left corner down at a 90-degree angle, the third number tells you where to mark and then fold the right corner down at a 90-degree angle.

Sheet	Left Fold	Right Fold
1	16.3	16.8
2	15.9	17.1
3	15.8	17.4
4	3.1	4.5
5	15.5	17.7
6	3.0	5.3
7	15.4	17.9
8	3.0	5.8
9	15.3	18.1
10	3.1	6.3
11	15.3	18.2
12	3.3	6.6
13	14.7	18.3
14	3.4	7.0
15	14.1	18.3
16	3.5	7.3

17	13.8	18.3
18	3.6	7.7
19	10.4	11.0
20	13.3	18.3
------	------	------
21	3.9	8.1
22	9.9	11.5
23	13.0	18.2
24	4.1	8.5
25	9.7	11.8
------	------	------
26	12.8	18.1
27	4.4	8.8
28	9.6	11.9
29	12.6	18.4
30	4.7	9.1
------	------	------
31	12.5	18.5
32	5.0	12.1
33	12.4	18.6
34	5.2	12.3
35	5.4	18.7
------	------	------
36	5.5	18.7
37	5.7	18.8
38	5.8	18.8
39	6.0	18.8
40	6.2	18.8
------	------	------
41	6.4	18.9
42	6.6	16.9

| 43 | 17.7 | 18.9 |
| 44 | 7.1 | 16.5 |
45	17.9	18.9
46	7.7	16.4
47	18.1	19.0
48	8.2	16.3
49	18.1	19.0
50	8.2	16.2
51	18.2	19.0
52	8.1	16.2
53	18.1	19.0
54	8.1	16.2
55	18.2	19.0
56	7.4	16.2
57	18.1	19.0
58	6.9	16.3
59	18.0	19.0
60	6.4	16.5
61	17.9	18.9
62	5.9	16.6
63	17.6	18.9
64	5.5	18.9
65	5.3	18.8
66	5.1	18.8
67	4.9	18.8
68	4.7	18.7

69	4.5	18.7
70	4.4	18.6

71	12.3	18.6
72	4.0	8.8
73	9.1	12.0
74	12.5	18.4
75	3.6	8.4

76	9.5	11.9
77	12.7	18.3
78	3.2	8.0
79	9.7	11.8
80	12.9	18.1

81	3.1	7.5
82	9.9	11.6
83	13.2	18.3
84	3.2	7.0
85	10.4	11.1

86	3.3	6.5
87	13.7	18.3
88	3.4	6.2
89	14.1	18.3
90	3.6	6.3

91	14.6	18.3
92	3.7	6.3
93	15.3	18.2
94	3.9	6.4

95	15.3	18.1

96	4.1	6.4
97	15.4	17.9
98	4.3	6.4
99	15.5	17.7
100	4.6	6.5

101	15.6	17.5
102	4.9	6.5
103	15.9	17.1
104	5.2	6.5
105	5.4	6.5

106	5.6	6.5
107	5.8	6.5
108	6.1	6.5
109	6.4	6.5

Now that you finished marking- FOLD and add a *cotton*tail!

Remember! When left or right folded paper is too long to lay flat because it extends beyond the book spine use scissors. Simply trim the excess in a straight line from page edge toward book spine and gently tear off the excess.

MyChicArt Folding Pattern for **Harvest Pumpkin 226 Folds**

==

Instructions:
These measurements describe where to mark and fold the pages of your 22cm or longer book with at least 452-page numbers. All measurements are given in cm. The first number indicates the sheet number (2-page numbers equals one sheet, the second tells you where (measured with a metric ruler placed at the left edge of the page at the '0' mark) to mark and then fold the left corner down at a 90-degree angle; the third number tells you where to mark and then fold the right corner down at a 90 degree angle. Each set of 5 sheets is separated by a line in this pattern to help keep your place as you mark pages.

Sheet	Left Fold	Right Fold
1	12.0	14.2
2	11.6	14.6
3	11.3	14.9
4	11.1	15.2
5	10.8	15.4
6	10.7	15.6
7	10.5	15.8
8	10.3	16.0
9	10.2	16.1
10	10.1	16.3
11	9.9	16.4
12	9.7	16.6
13	9.6	16.7
14	9.5	16.8
15	9.4	16.9

16	9.3	17.0
17	9.2	17.1
18	9.1	17.2
19	9.0	17.3
20	8.9	17.4
--		
21	14.4	17.4
22	8.7	11.9
23	15.2	17.6
24	8.6	11.4
25	15.7	17.7
--		
26	8.5	11.0
27	16.1	17.7
28	12.8	13.5
29	8.3	10.5
30	16.6	17.9
--		
31	11.5	14.9
32	8.2	10.1
33	17.0	18.0
34	10.9	15.7
35	8.0	9.8
--		
36	17.4	18.0
37	10.5	16.3
38	7.9	9.5
39	17.7	18.1
40	10.1	16.9
--		
41	7.8	9.2

42	18.0	18.1
43	9.8	17.3
44	7.7	8.8
45	9.4	17.6
46	7.6	8.6
47	9.2	17.8
48	7.6	8.5
49	9.0	17.9
50	7.6	8.3
51	8.9	18.0
52	7.6	8.2
53	8.7	18.1
54	7.5	8.0
55	8.5	18.3
56	7.5	7.8
57	4.4	4.6
58	8.3	18.4
59	7.5	7.7
60	4.3	4.6
61	8.1	18.5
62	4.2	4.5
63	8.0	18.6
64	4.2	4.5
65	7.9	18.6
66	4.1	4.5
67	7.8	18.7

68	4.1	4.5
69	7.7	18.8
70	4.0	4.4
- -		
71	13.1	18.8
72	7.6	11.7
73	5.3	6.5
74	4.0	4.4
75	15.7	18.9
- -		
76	7.6	10.3
77	4.9	6.8
78	4.0	4.4
79	16.8	18.9
80	12.0	14.7
- -		
81	7.5	9.1
82	6.6	7.0
83	4.0	5.1
84	17.7	18.9
85	10.3	16.2
- -		
86	7.6	8.4
87	6.7	7.0
88	4.1	4.9
89	18.4	18.9
90	9.2	17.2
- -		
91	7.7	7.8
92	6.5	7.0
93	4.1	5.1

94	8.5	17.8
95	4.2	6.9
-----	-----	-----
96	8.3	18.0
97	4.2	6.7
98	8.1	18.2
99	4.2	6.5
100	8.0	18.4
-----	-----	-----
101	4.3	4.7
102	7.8	18.6
103	4.3	4.8
104	7.6	18.8
105	4.4	4.9
-----	-----	-----
106	7.5	18.8
107	4.4	5.0
108	7.4	18.9
109	4.5	5.1
110	7.4	18.9
-----	-----	-----
111	4.5	5.2
112	7.4	19.0
113	4.6	5.7
114	7.3	19.0
115	4.7	7.1
-----	-----	-----
116	7.3	19.0
117	4.9	7.1
118	7.3	19.0
119	5.1	7.1

120	7.3	18.9
----	----	----
121	5.3	7.2
122	7.4	18.9
123	5.6	7.2
124	7.4	18.8
125	6.0	7.2
----	----	----
126	7.5	18.7
127	6.8	7.3
128	7.5	18.7
129	7.6	18.6
130	7.6	18.5
----	----	----
131	7.6	18.5
132	7.7	18.4
133	7.8	18.3
134	7.9	18.2
135	8.0	18.1
----	----	----
136	8.0	18.0
137	8.1	17.9
138	8.3	17.6
139	7.7	7.9
140	18.4	18.9
----	----	----
141	8.7	17.1
142	7.6	8.3
143	18.0	18.9
144	9.3	16.6
145	7.6	8.7

146	17.5	18.9
147	9.9	15.9
148	7.5	9.1
149	17.0	18.9
150	10.9	15.0

151	7.5	9.6
152	16.4	18.9
153	7.5	10.0
154	16.0	18.9
155	7.6	10.5

156	15.4	18.8
157	7.6	11.2
158	7.7	18.8
159	7.7	18.8
160	7.7	18.7

161	7.7	18.7
162	7.8	18.7
163	7.9	18.7
164	7.9	18.6
165	8.0	18.6

166	8.1	18.5
167	7.5	7.6
168	8.2	18.4
169	7.5	7.7
170	8.4	18.4

171	7.5	7.8
172	8.5	18.3
173	7.5	8.0
174	8.8	18.1
175	7.6	8.3
--		
176	9.0	18.0
177	7.6	8.4
178	9.1	17.8
179	7.6	8.5
180	9.3	17.7
--		
181	7.7	8.7
182	9.5	17.5
183	7.7	8.9
184	9.7	17.4
185	7.8	9.1
--		
186	17.9	18.1
187	10.1	16.9
188	7.9	9.4
189	17.6	18.1
190	10.5	16.3
--		
191	8.0	9.7
192	17.3	18.0
193	10.9	15.7
194	8.1	10.0
195	16.9	17.9
--		
196	11.5	14.9

197	8.3	10.4
198	16.5	17.8
199	12.8	13.5
200	8.4	10.8

201	15.9	17.7
202	8.5	11.2
203	15.5	17.6
204	8.7	11.6
205	14.9	17.5

206	8.8	12.3
207	8.9	17.4
208	9.0	17.3
209	9.1	17.2
210	9.2	17.1

211	9.3	17.0
212	9.4	16.9
213	9.5	16.8
214	9.6	16.7
215	9.7	16.6

216	9.8	16.5
217	9.9	16.4
218	10.1	16.3
219	10.3	16.0
220	10.5	15.8

221	10.7	15.6

222	10.8	15.4
223	11.1	15.2
224	11.3	14.9
225	11.6	14.6
- -		
226	12.0	14.2

Now that you have marked all the Sheets- HAVE FUN FOLDING!

Remember! When left or right folded paper is too long to lay flat because it extends beyond the book spine use scissors. Simply trim the excess in a straight line from page edge toward book spine and gently tear off the excess. The amount trimmed can be wider than is necessary to prevent the fold extending beyond the book spine. The width you choose to trim will not affect the look of the completed book.

MyChicArt Book Folding Pattern for **Football 150 Folds**

===

Instructions:

These measurements describe where to fold the pages of your 20cm or larger book with at least 300 pages. All measurements are given in cm. The first number indicates the sheet number (2-page numbers equals one sheet), the second tells you where (measured with a cm ruler placed at the left edge of the page at the '0' mark) to mark and fold the left corner down at a 90 degree angle; the third tells you where to mark and fold the right corner down at a 90 degree angle.

Sheet	Left Fold	Right Fold
1	13.8	15.0
2	13.6	15.2
3	13.4	15.4
4	13.3	15.6
5	13.4	15.8
6	13.5	15.9
7	13.6	16.0
8	11.7	12.2
9	13.7	16.1
10	11.3	12.3
11	13.9	16.3
12	10.9	12.4
13	14.0	16.3
14	10.6	12.6
15	14.2	16.4

16	10.3	12.7
17	14.3	16.4
18	10.0	12.9
19	14.4	16.5
20	9.7	13.0
---	---	---
21	14.6	16.5
22	9.5	13.2
23	14.7	16.5
24	9.3	13.3
25	14.9	16.5
---	---	---
26	9.0	13.5
27	15.0	16.5
28	8.8	13.6
29	15.2	16.6
30	8.7	13.8
---	---	---
31	15.3	16.6
32	8.5	13.9
33	15.5	16.6
34	8.3	14.1
35	15.6	16.5
---	---	---
36	8.2	14.2
37	15.8	16.5
38	8.0	14.4
39	15.9	16.5
40	7.9	14.5

----	----	----
41	16.1	16.5
42	7.8	14.7
43	16.2	16.5
44	7.7	14.8
45	16.4	16.4
----	----	----
46	7.5	12.2
47	12.6	15.0
48	7.4	12.1
49	12.7	15.2
50	7.3	12.2
----	----	----
51	12.9	15.3
52	7.2	12.3
53	13.0	15.5
54	7.1	12.4
55	13.2	15.6
----	----	----
56	11.6	12.2
57	13.3	15.8
58	6.9	11.3
59	11.9	12.0
60	13.3	16.0
----	----	----
61	6.8	11.4
62	12.4	13.1
63	12.3	16.1
64	6.7	11.6

65	12.3	16.1

66	6.6	11.5
67	6.6	10.7
68	10.9	11.3
69	12.6	16.0
70	6.5	10.5

71	11.8	12.2
72	12.4	15.9
73	11.6	15.9
74	6.4	10.8
75	11.5	15.9

76	6.3	10.8
77	11.6	15.8
78	11.7	15.8
79	6.2	9.8
80	11.1	11.2

81	11.8	15.7
82	6.1	9.8
83	10.9	11.4
84	6.1	9.9
85	10.7	15.6

86	6.0	10.0
87	10.7	15.5
88	6.0	9.1

89	9.3	9.8
90	10.9	15.3
---	---	---
91	9.4	9.7
92	10.2	10.5
93	10.9	15.2
94	6.3	9.1
95	10.0	15.2
---	---	---
96	6.5	9.2
97	9.9	15.1
98	6.6	9.3
99	10.0	15.0
100	6.8	9.5
---	---	---
101	10.2	14.9
102	6.9	9.6
103	10.1	14.8
104	7.0	9.8
105	7.1	14.7
---	---	---
106	7.2	14.6
107	7.3	14.6
108	5.7	5.8
109	7.4	14.4
110	5.7	6.0
---	---	---
111	7.6	14.3
112	5.6	6.2

113	7.7	14.2
114	5.6	6.3
115	7.9	14.0
116	5.6	6.4
117	8.0	13.9
118	5.6	6.6
119	8.2	13.7
120	5.6	6.7
121	8.3	13.6
122	5.6	6.9
123	8.4	13.4
124	5.6	7.0
125	8.6	13.2
126	5.6	7.2
127	8.7	13.0
128	5.6	7.3
129	8.9	12.8
130	5.6	7.5
131	9.0	12.5
132	5.7	7.6
132	9.2	12.3
133	5.7	7.8
134	9.3	12.0
135	5.7	7.9

137	9.5	11.7
138	5.8	8.1
139	9.6	11.4
140	5.8	8.2
------	------	------
141	9.8	11.1
142	5.9	8.4
143	9.9	10.7
144	6.1	8.5
145	10.1	10.2
------	------	------
146	6.3	8.7
147	6.3	8.7
148	6.5	8.8
149	6.7	8.8
150	7.2	8.3

When Folded add your favorite Team's Ribbon Color to hold back extra pages!

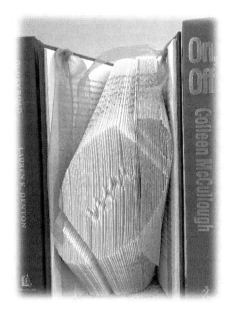

Pattern copyright of MyChicArt- Not for distribution or resale

==

Instructions:

These measurements describe where to mark and fold the pages of your 20cm or longer book with at least 416-page numbers. All measurements are given in cm. Position your hardcover book horizontally (with the spine closest to you.)The first number indicates the sheet number (2-page numbers equals one sheet; the second tells you where (measured with a metric ruler placed at the left edge of the page at the '0' mark) to mark and then fold the left corner down at a 90 degree angle; the third number tells you where to mark and then fold the right corner down at a 90 degree angle.

Sheet	Left Fold	Right Fold
1	8.9	10.4
2	8.6	10.7
3	8.4	10.9
4	8.2	11.2
5	8.0	11.3
6	7.8	11.5
7	7.7	11.6
8	7.6	11.7
9	7.5	11.8
10	7.4	11.9
11	7.3	12.1
12	7.2	12.2
13	7.1	12.2
14	7.0	12.3
15	6.9	12.4

16	6.8	12.5
17	6.8	12.6
18	6.7	12.6
19	6.7	12.7
20	6.6	12.8

21	6.5	12.9
22	6.5	9.1
23	10.5	13.0
24	6.4	8.7
25	10.8	13.2

26	6.3	8.4
27	11.0	13.4
28	6.2	8.3
29	11.2	13.5
30	6.2	8.1

31	11.3	13.7
32	6.1	8.0
33	11.5	13.8
34	6.1	7.9
35	11.7	14.0

36	6.0	7.8
37	11.8	14.2
38	6.0	7.7
39	12.0	14.3
40	6.0	7.7

41	12.2	14.5
42	5.9	7.6
43	12.3	14.7
44	5.9	7.6
45	12.5	14.8

46	5.9	7.6
47	12.6	15.0
48	5.8	7.6
49	12.8	15.1
50	5.5	7.6

51	13.0	15.3
52	5.2	7.6
53	13.1	15.5
54	5.0	7.7
55	13.3	15.6

56	4.8	7.7
57	13.4	15.8
58	4.7	7.8
59	13.6	15.9
60	4.5	7.8

61	13.8	16.1
62	4.4	8.0
63	13.9	16.3
64	4.3	8.1
65	14.1	16.4

66	4.2	8.2
67	14.2	16.6
68	4.1	8.4
69	14.4	16.8
70	4.0	6.1

71	6.5	8.6
72	14.7	17.0
73	3.9	5.8
74	6.5	8.7
75	14.5	16.9

76	3.8	5.7
77	6.4	8.4
78	14.3	16.7
79	3.7	5.5
80	6.3	8.2

81	14.1	16.4
82	3.6	5.4
83	6.2	8.0
84	13.8	16.2
85	3.6	5.3

86	6.1	7.8
87	13.6	15.9
88	3.5	5.3
89	6.0	7.7
90	13.3	15.7

91	3.5	5.2
92	6.0	7.7
93	13.1	15.4
94	3.5	5.2
95	6.0	7.6

96	12.9	15.2
97	3.5	5.2
98	6.0	7.6
99	12.6	15.0
100	3.5	5.2

101	6.0	7.6
102	12.4	14.7
103	3.5	5.3
104	6.0	7.6
105	12.1	14.7

106	3.6	5.3
107	6.0	7.7
108	11.9	14.9
109	3.6	5.5
110	6.1	7.8

111	11.7	15.1
112	3.7	5.6
113	6.2	7.9
114	11.4	15.4
115	3.8	5.8

116	6.3	8.1
117	11.2	15.6
118	3.9	6.0
119	6.4	8.3
120	4.0	6.1

121	6.5	8.6
122	10.6	13.1
123	13.7	16.1
124	4.2	6.5
125	6.7	12.8

126	13.7	16.1
127	4.1	6.3
128	6.8	12.6
129	13.5	15.9
130	4.0	6.1

131	7.1	12.4
132	13.2	15.7
133	3.9	5.9
134	7.3	12.1
135	13.0	15.4

136	3.8	5.7
137	7.6	11.8
138	12.8	15.2
139	3.7	5.5
140	8.1	11.3

141	12.5	14.9
142	3.6	5.4
143	8.7	10.7
144	12.3	14.7
145	12.2	14.6
146	3.6	5.3
147	12.0	14.4
148	3.5	5.3
149	11.9	14.3
150	3.5	5.2
151	11.7	14.1
152	3.5	5.2
153	11.6	14.0
154	3.5	5.2
155	11.4	13.8
156	3.5	5.2
157	11.2	13.6
158	3.5	5.2
159	11.1	13.5
160	3.5	5.2
161	10.9	13.3
162	3.5	5.3
163	10.8	13.2
164	3.5	5.3
165	10.6	13.0

166	3.6	5.3
167	10.4	12.8
168	3.6	5.4
169	10.3	12.7
170	3.7	5.5

171	10.1	12.5
172	3.7	5.6
173	9.9	12.4
174	3.8	5.7
175	9.8	12.2

176	3.8	5.8
177	9.6	12.0
178	3.9	6.0
179	9.5	11.9
180	4.0	6.1

181	9.3	11.7
182	4.1	6.3
183	9.0	11.6
184	4.2	6.6
185	8.7	11.4

186	4.3	7.0
187	8.1	11.2
188	4.4	11.2
189	4.5	11.1
190	4.5	11.0

191	4.6	10.9
192	4.7	10.8
193	4.7	10.8
194	4.8	10.7
195	4.9	10.6
--		
196	5.0	10.5
197	5.1	10.4
198	5.2	10.3
199	5.3	10.2
200	5.4	10.1
--		
201	5.6	9.9
202	5.7	9.8
203	5.8	9.6
204	6.0	9.5
205	6.2	9.3
--		
206	6.4	9.1
207	6.7	8.8
208	7.1	8.4

Now that you have marked all the Sheets- FOLD and share your love!

Remember! When left or right folded paper is too long to lay flat because it extends beyond the book spine use scissors. Simply trim the excess in a straight line from page edge toward book spine and gently tear off the excess. The amount trimmed can be wider than is necessary to prevent the fold extending beyond the book spine. The width you choose to trim will not affect the look of the completed book.

===

Instructions:
These measurements describe where to mark and fold the pages of your 20cm or longer book with at least 314-page numbers. All measurements are given in cm. The first number indicates the sheet number (2-page numbers equals one sheet, the second tells you where (measured with a metric ruler placed at the left edge of the page at the '0' mark) to mark and then fold the left corner down at a 90-degree angle; the third number tells you where to mark and then fold the right corner down at a 90 degree angle.

Sheet	Left Fold	Right Fold
1	16.7	16.7
2	16.5	16.8
3	16.4	16.8
4	16.3	16.8
5	16.2	16.8
6	16.1	16.8
7	15.9	16.8
8	15.8	16.8
9	15.7	16.8
10	15.6	16.8
11	15.4	16.8
12	15.3	16.8
13	12.7	13.0
14	15.1	16.8
15	12.4	13.0
16	14.8	16.8

17	12.2	13.0
18	14.5	16.8
19	12.0	13.0
20	14.3	16.8

21	11.7	13.0
22	14.0	16.8
23	11.4	13.0
24	13.8	16.8
25	11.2	13.0

26	13.5	16.8
27	8.6	9.0
28	10.8	13.0
29	13.2	16.8
30	8.3	9.0

31	10.4	13.0
32	13.2	16.8
33	7.9	9.0
34	10.0	13.0
35	13.2	16.8

36	7.6	9.0
37	9.6	13.0
38	13.2	16.8
39	7.2	9.0
40	9.3	13.0

41	13.2	16.8

42	6.8	9.0
43	9.2	13.0
44	13.2	16.8
45	6.5	9.0
--		
46	9.2	13.0
47	13.2	16.8
48	6.2	9.0
49	9.2	13.0
50	13.2	16.8
--		
51	5.8	9.0
52	9.2	13.0
53	13.2	16.8
54	5.5	9.0
55	9.2	13.0
--		
56	13.2	16.8
57	5.1	9.0
58	17.0	18.6
59	4.9	9.0
60	9.2	13.0
--		
61	13.2	16.8
62	17.0	18.7
63	4.4	9.0
64	9.2	13.0
65	13.2	16.8
--		
66	17.0	18.7

67	3.9	9.0
68	9.2	13.0
69	13.2	16.8
70	17.0	18.7

71	3.5	9.0
72	9.2	13.0
73	13.2	16.8
74	17.0	18.7
75	3.0	9.0

76	9.2	13.0
77	13.2	16.8
78	17.0	18.7
79	2.8	9.0
80	9.2	13.0

81	13.2	16.8
82	17.0	18.7
83	3.2	9.0
84	9.2	13.0
85	13.2	16.8

86	17.0	18.7
87	3.6	9.0
88	9.2	13.0
89	13.2	16.8
90	17.0	18.7

91	4.0	9.0

92	9.2	13.0
93	13.2	16.8
94	17.0	18.7
95	4.5	9.0
---	---	---
96	9.2	13.0
97	13.2	16.8
98	17.0	18.7
99	5.0	9.0
100	9.2	13.0
---	---	---
101	13.2	16.8
102	5.3	9.0
103	9.2	13.0
104	13.2	16.8
105	5.7	9.0
---	---	---
106	9.2	13.0
107	13.2	16.8
108	6.0	9.0
109	9.2	13.0
110	13.2	16.8
---	---	---
111	6.3	9.0
112	9.2	13.0
113	13.2	16.8
114	6.7	9.0
115	9.2	13.0
---	---	---
116	13.2	16.8

117	7.0	9.0
118	9.3	13.0
119	13.2	16.8
120	7.3	9.0

121	9.7	13.0
122	13.2	16.8
123	7.7	9.0
124	10.1	13.0
125	13.2	16.8

126	8.0	9.0
127	10.5	13.0
128	13.2	16.8
129	8.4	9.0
130	10.8	13.0

131	13.4	16.8
132	8.7	9.0
133	11.2	13.0
134	13.8	16.8
135	11.4	13.0

136	14.1	16.8
137	11.7	13.0
138	14.3	16.8
139	11.9	13.0
140	14.6	16.8

| 141 | 12.2 | 13.0 |

142	14.8	16.8
143	12.4	13.0
144	15.1	16.8
145	12.7	13.0
-------	-------	-------
146	15.3	16.8
147	15.4	16.8
148	15.5	16.8
149	15.7	16.8
150	15.8	16.8
-------	-------	-------
151	15.9	16.8
152	16.1	16.8
153	16.2	16.8
154	16.3	16.8
155	16.4	16.8
-------	-------	-------
156	16.5	16.8
157	16.7	16.7

Now that you have marked all the Sheets- **HAVE FUN FOLDING and Decorating!**

This Pattern requires the trimming some of the pages due to multiple layers in the design. This step will allow for sheets of paper to lay flat and not extend beyond the book spine when folded. When the Left Fold pattern number begins with 14,15,16 you will need to use scissors to cut the sheet (page edge toward spine) and gently tear off close to the spine. It is suggested that all cutting be done after all pages are marked and before folding begins.

MyChicArt Book Folding Art Pattern for **Angel** <u>**170 Folds**</u>

===

Instructions:

These measurements describe where to mark and fold the pages of your 22cm or longer book with at least 340-page numbers. All measurements are given in cm. The first number indicates the sheet number (2-page numbers equals one sheet, the second tells you where (measured with a metric ruler placed at the left edge of the page at the '0' mark) to mark and then fold the left corner down at a 90-degree angle; the third number tells you where to mark and then fold the right corner down at a 90-degree angle.

Sheet	Left Fold	Right Fold
1	8.1	8.5
2	6.9	7.2
3	8.0	8.8
4	6.6	7.5
5	7.9	8.9
6	6.6	7.7
7	6.6	9.0
8	6.6	9.1
9	9.4	10.1
10	6.6	10.2
11	6.6	10.3
12	5.5	10.3
13	5.3	10.4
14	5.1	10.4
15	5.0	10.5
16	4.9	10.5
17	4.8	10.5

18	4.8	10.5
19	4.9	10.5
20	5.3	10.5
21	5.7	10.5
22	6.0	10.5
23	6.2	10.5
24	6.4	10.5
25	6.5	10.5
26	6.7	10.5
27	10.7	11.3
28	6.9	11.4
29	7.0	11.5
30	7.1	11.6
31	7.2	11.6
32	7.2	11.6
33	18.1	18.4
34	7.3	11.6
35	17.9	18.6
36	7.5	11.7
37	17.7	18.7
38	7.6	11.6
39	17.5	18.7
40	7.7	11.6
41	17.2	18.8
42	7.8	11.6

43	16.7	18.9
44	7.8	11.5
45	16.3	18.9
46	7.9	11.4
47	15.9	18.9
48	8.0	11.4
49	15.3	19.0
50	8.0	12.0
51	14.8	19.0
52	8.1	12.1
53	14.4	19.1
54	8.1	12.2
55	13.1	19.1
56	8.2	12.3
57	13.3	19.1
58	8.2	12.3
59	12.9	19.1
60	8.2	12.3
61	12.5	19.1
62	8.3	19.1
63	8.3	19.2
64	6.4	7.4
65	8.3	19.2
66	6.0	7.6
67	8.2	19.2

68	5.7	7.7
69	8.1	19.2
70	5.6	7.9
---	---	---
71	8.0	19.2
72	5.5	8.0
73	5.4	19.2
74	5.3	19.2
75	5.3	19.2
---	---	---
76	5.3	19.3
77	5.2	19.3
78	5.2	19.3
79	5.1	19.3
80	5.1	19.3
---	---	---
81	5.1	19.3
82	5.1	19.3
83	5.1	19.3
84	5.1	19.3
85	5.1	19.3
---	---	---
86	5.1	19.3
87	5.1	19.3
88	5.1	19.3
89	5.1	19.3
90	5.1	19.3
---	---	---
91	5.1	19.3
92	5.1	19.3

93	5.2	19.3
94	5.2	19.3
95	5.2	19.3
---	---	---
96	5.3	19.2
97	5.3	19.2
98	5.4	19.2
99	5.4	19.2
100	5.5	7.9
---	---	---
101	8.1	19.2
102	5.6	7.8
103	8.1	19.2
104	5.8	7.7
105	8.2	19.2
---	---	---
106	6.1	7.5
107	8.3	19.2
108	6.4	7.4
109	8.3	19.1
110	8.3	12.3
---	---	---
111	12.7	19.1
112	8.2	12.3
113	13.1	19.1
114	8.2	12.3
115	13.6	19.1
---	---	---
116	8.2	12.3
117	14.1	19.1

118	8.1	12.2
119	14.6	19.1
120	8.1	12.1
---	---	---
121	15.0	19.0
122	8.0	11.9
123	15.5	19.0
124	7.9	11.4
125	16.1	18.9
---	---	---
126	7.9	11.5
127	16.5	18.9
128	7.8	11.5
129	16.9	18.8
130	7.7	11.6
---	---	---
131	17.3	18.8
132	7.6	11.6
133	17.6	18.7
134	7.5	11.7
135	17.8	18.6
---	---	---
136	7.4	11.7
137	17.9	18.5
138	7.3	11.6
139	7.3	11.6
140	7.2	11.6
---	---	---
141	7.1	11.6
142	7.0	11.5

143	6.9	11.4
144	6.8	10.6
145	10.8	11.2

146	6.6	10.5
147	6.4	10.5
148	6.3	10.5
149	6.1	10.5
150	5.8	10.5

151	5.4	10.5
152	4.9	10.5
153	4.8	10.5
154	4.8	10.5
155	4.9	10.5

156	4.9	10.5
157	5.1	10.4
158	5.3	10.4
159	5.5	10.3
160	6.6	10.3

161	6.6	10.2
162	6.6	9.2
163	9.5	10.0
164	6.6	9.1
165	7.9	9.0

166	6.6	7.6
167	7.9	8.9
168	6.7	7.4
169	8.0	8.7
170	8.1	8.5

Find a Special word on a book page and use it for your Angel's Halo!

==
Instructions:

These measurements describe where to mark and fold the pages of your 20cm or larger book with at least 278-page numbers. All measurements are given in cm. The first number indicates the sheet number (2-page numbers equals one sheet); the second tells you where (measured with a cm ruler placed at the left edge of the page at the '0' mark) to mark and then fold the left corner down at a 90-degree angle, the third number tells you where to mark and then fold the right corner down at a 90-degree angle.

Sheet	Left Fold	Right Fold
1	13.1	14.1
2	12.9	14.3
3	12.6	14.6
4	12.3	14.9
5	12.2	15.0
6	11.9	15.3
7	11.8	15.4
8	11.6	15.6
9	11.5	15.7
10	11.4	15.8
11	11.3	15.9
12	11.2	16.0
13	11.1	16.1
14	11.0	16.2
15	10.9	16.3
16	10.8	16.4

17	10.7	16.4
18	7.8	9.3
19	10.6	16.6
20	10.5	13.0
21	14.5	16.7
22	7.0	10.0
23	10.2	12.3
24	6.8	12.2
25	15.1	17.0
26	6.6	11.9
27	15.3	17.1
28	6.4	11.7
29	15.6	17.2
30	6.2	11.5
31	15.7	17.3
32	9.1	11.4
33	15.8	17.4
34	3.4	5.4
35	5.9	7.4
36	16.0	17.5
37	3.0	7.2
38	10.0	11.3
39	16.2	17.6
40	2.7	6.9

41	10.3	11.4
42	16.3	17.7
43	2.5	6.6
44	10.4	11.6
45	16.4	17.8

46	2.3	3.7
47	5.2	6.5
48	10.7	11.7
49	16.6	17.9
50	2.1	3.2

51	5.6	6.7
52	10.8	11.8
53	16.7	17.9
54	1.9	2.9
55	5.8	6.8

56	10.9	11.9
57	16.8	18.0
58	1.8	2.8
59	6.0	6.9
60	11.0	12.0

61	16.8	18.0
62	1.7	2.6
63	6.1	7.0
64	11.1	12.0
65	16.8	18.0

66	1.7	2.5
67	6.2	7.1
68	11.1	12.0
69	16.9	18.1
70	1.6	2.5

71	6.2	7.1
72	11.1	12.0
73	16.9	18.0
74	1.6	2.4
75	6.2	7.1

76	11.1	12.0
77	16.8	18.0
78	1.6	2.5
79	6.2	7.0
80	11.0	12.0

81	16.8	18.0
82	1.7	2.5
83	6.1	7.0
84	10.9	11.9
85	16.7	17.9

86	1.7	2.6
87	6.0	6.9
88	10.8	11.8
89	16.6	17.9
90	1.8	2.8

91	5.8	6.8
92	10.7	11.8
93	16.5	17.8
94	1.9	3.0
95	5.5	6.7

96	10.5	11.6
97	16.4	17.7
98	2.1	3.3
99	5.2	6.5
100	10.3	11.5

101	16.2	17.6
102	2.3	4.0
103	2.4	6.7
104	10.0	11.3
105	16.0	17.4

106	2.6	6.9
107	9.7	11.2
108	15.8	17.3
109	2.9	7.3
110	3.0	5.6

111	5.9	7.7
112	8.9	11.3
113	6.0	11.4
114	15.3	17.0
115	6.3	11.7

116	15.0	16.9
117	6.5	11.9
118	14.7	16.8
119	6.7	12.2
120	6.8	10.0

121	10.3	12.7
122	13.7	16.5
123	7.3	9.5
124	10.5	16.3
125	7.8	9.0

126	10.7	16.2
127	10.8	16.1
128	10.9	16.0
129	11.0	15.9
130	11.1	15.8

131	11.2	15.7
132	11.3	15.5
133	11.4	15.4
134	11.6	15.2
135	11.7	15.1

136	11.9	14.9
137	12.1	14.8
138	12.3	14.5
139	12.6	14.2

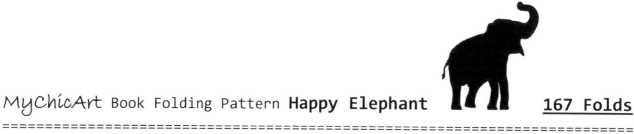
===

Instructions:

These measurements describe where to mark and fold the pages of your 23cm or larger book with at least 334-page numbers. All measurements are given in cm. The first number indicates the sheet number (2-page numbers equals one sheet); the second tells you where (measured with a cm ruler placed at the left edge of the page at the '0' mark) to mark and then fold the left corner down at a 90 degree angle, the third number tells you where to mark and then fold the right corner down at a 90 degree angle.

Sheet	Left Fold	Right Fold
1	13.3	13.4
2	12.7	13.4
3	12.7	13.3
4	12.1	13.3
5	11.8	13.2
6	11.6	13.1
7	11.5	12.0
8	11.4	11.9
9	11.2	11.8
10	11.1	11.8
11	11.0	11.7
12	10.9	11.7
13	10.6	12.5
14	10.3	13.1
15	10.1	13.6

16	10.0	13.9
17	9.9	14.1
18	16.3	16.9
19	9.7	14.7
20	9.6	17.0
------	------	------
21	9.6	17.0
22	9.5	17.0
23	9.4	17.0
24	9.4	17.0
25	9.3	17.0
------	------	------
26	9.3	17.0
27	9.2	17.0
28	9.1	17.0
29	9.1	17.0
30	9.0	17.0
------	------	------
31	9.0	17.0
32	8.9	17.0
33	8.9	15.9
34	16.5	17.0
35	8.8	14.2
------	------	------
36	16.9	16.9
37	8.7	14.1
38	8.7	14.1
39	8.7	14.1
40	8.6	14.1
------	------	------

41	8.6	14.1
42	15.9	16.6
43	8.5	13.9
44	15.3	16.7
45	8.5	14.0
---	---	---
46	15.0	16.7
47	8.4	14.3
48	8.4	16.7
49	8.4	16.7
50	8.3	16.7
---	---	---
51	8.3	16.7
52	8.3	16.7
53	8.3	16.7
54	8.2	16.7
55	8.2	16.7
---	---	---
56	8.2	16.7
57	8.2	16.7
58	16.1	16.7
59	8.1	15.6
60	8.1	15.3
---	---	---
61	8.0	15.1
62	8.0	14.9
63	8.0	14.7
64	8.0	14.6
65	7.9	14.5

66	7.9	14.4
67	7.9	14.3
68	7.9	14.2
69	7.9	14.2
70	7.9	14.1
---	---	---
71	7.9	14.0
72	7.8	13.9
73	7.8	13.9
74	7.8	13.8
75	7.7	13.8
---	---	---
76	7.6	13.7
77	7.5	13.7
78	7.4	13.6
79	7.0	13.6
80	16.5	16.8
---	---	---
81	6.7	13.6
82	16.2	16.9
83	6.6	13.9
84	15.7	16.9
85	6.6	14.3
---	---	---
86	14.8	17.0
87	6.6	16.9
88	6.5	16.9
89	6.5	16.9
90	6.4	16.9

91	6.3	16.9
92	6.2	17.0
93	6.2	17.0
94	6.1	17.0
95	6.1	17.0
---	---	---
96	16.6	17.0
97	6.1	16.0
98	6.1	15.7
99	6.1	13.8
100	6.1	13.9
---	---	---
101	6.1	14.4
102	16.1	16.9
103	6.1	15.3
104	6.1	16.9
105	6.1	16.9
---	---	---
106	6.1	16.9
107	6.1	16.9
108	6.1	16.9
109	6.1	16.9
110	6.1	16.9
---	---	---
111	6.1	16.9
112	6.1	16.9
113	6.1	12.2
114	13.2	16.9
115	6.1	11.0
---	---	---

116	13.9	16.9
117	15.0	16.9
118	6.2	10.3
119	6.2	10.3
120	6.2	10.3
121	6.2	10.3
122	6.3	10.3
123	6.3	10.2
124	6.3	10.2
125	6.3	10.2
126	6.3	10.2
127	6.3	10.2
128	6.3	10.2
129	6.3	10.2
130	6.4	10.2
131	4.2	4.9
132	6.4	10.2
133	4.1	5.0
134	6.4	10.2
135	4.0	5.1
136	6.5	10.2
137	4.1	5.1
138	6.5	8.5
139	9.4	10.4
140	4.2	5.1

141	6.5	8.5
142	10.0	10.5
143	4.3	5.1
144	6.5	8.5
145	4.3	5.1

146	6.5	8.5
147	4.4	5.2
148	6.4	8.5
149	4.4	5.2
150	6.2	8.4

151	4.4	5.4
152	4.4	8.3
153	4.4	8.2
154	4.5	8.2
155	4.5	8.1

156	4.5	8.0
157	4.6	7.9
158	4.6	7.8
159	4.7	7.7
160	4.7	7.6

161	4.8	7.5
162	4.9	7.4
163	5.0	7.2
164	5.1	7.1
165	5.2	6.9

166	5.4	6.7
167	5.7	6.3

This is one Happy Elephant- Trunk up 'Good Luck' HAPPY FOLDING!
Remember! For sheets that extend beyond the book spine trim the excess in a straight line from page edge toward book spine and gently tear off the excess.

Pattern copyright of MyChicArt- Not for distribution or resale

MyChicArt Book Folding Pattern **Harry Potter 211 Folds**

===

Instructions:

These measurements describe where to mark and fold the pages of your 22cm or longer book with at least 422-page numbers. All measurements are given in cm. The first number indicates the sheet number (2-page numbers equals one sheet, the second tells you where (measured with a metric ruler placed at the left edge of the page at the '0' mark) to mark and then fold the left corner down at a 90-degree angle; the third number tells you where to mark and then fold the right corner down at a 90-degree angle.

Sheet	Left Fold	Right Fold
1	9.4	9.5
2	9.4	9.7
3	9.4	9.8
4	9.3	10.0
5	9.3	10.0
6	9.3	10.2
7	9.3	10.3
8	9.3	9.7
9	9.9	10.4
10	9.2	9.6
11	10.0	10.6
12	9.2	9.5
13	10.1	10.7
14	9.2	9.5
15	10.2	10.7
16	9.2	9.4
17	10.2	10.8

18	9.1	9.3
19	9.1	9.3
20	10.3	10.9
--		
21	14.9	15.1
22	4.9	5.0
23	10.4	11.0
24	14.8	15.1
25	4.9	5.1
--		
26	10.5	11.1
27	14.6	15.1
28	4.9	5.4
29	10.6	11.2
30	14.3	15.1
--		
31	13.9	15.1
32	4.9	15.1
33	4.9	15.1
34	4.9	15.1
35	4.9	15.1
--		
36	4.9	15.1
37	4.9	15.1
38	4.9	15.1
39	4.9	15.1
40	4.9	15.1
--		
41	4.9	15.1
42	4.9	15.1

43	4.9	15.1
44	4.9	15.1
45	4.9	15.1

46	4.9	15.1
47	4.9	15.1
48	4.9	15.2
49	4.9	15.1
50	4.9	15.1

51	4.9	15.2
52	4.8	15.2
53	4.8	15.2
54	4.8	15.2
55	4.8	15.2

56	4.8	15.2
57	4.8	15.2
58	4.8	15.2
59	8.9	15.2
60	11.5	15.2

61	4.8	5.1
62	10.3	11.1
63	14.9	15.2
64	10.3	11.1
65	15.1	15.3

66	10.2	11.0
67	15.2	15.3

68	10.1	11.0
69	10.1	10.9
70	10.0	10.9
--		
71	10.0	10.9
72	10.0	10.9
73	9.9	10.8
74	9.9	10.8
75	15.8	15.9
--		
76	9.8	10.8
77	15.7	16.0
78	9.7	10.7
79	4.3	4.4
80	9.6	10.6
--		
81	15.4	16.0
82	4.3	4.5
83	9.5	10.5
84	15.0	15.9
85	4.3	6.7
--		
86	4.3	11.0
87	4.3	15.9
88	4.3	15.9
89	4.3	15.9
90	4.3	15.9
--		
91	4.3	15.9
92	4.3	15.9

93	4.3	15.9
94	4.3	15.9
95	4.3	15.9
-------	-------	-------
96	4.3	15.9
97	4.3	16.0
98	4.3	16.0
99	4.3	16.0
100	4.3	16.0
-------	-------	-------
101	4.3	16.0
102	4.3	16.0
103	4.3	16.0
104	4.3	16.0
105	4.3	16.0
-------	-------	-------
106	4.3	16.0
107	4.3	16.0
108	4.3	16.0
109	4.3	16.0
110	4.3	16.0
-------	-------	-------
111	4.3	16.0
112	4.3	5.0
113	8.8	9.3
114	15.4	16.1
115	4.3	4.6
-------	-------	-------
116	8.7	9.2
117	15.8	16.1

118	4.3	4.3
119	15.9	16.1
120	8.7	9.1

121	15.9	16.1
122	8.7	9.1
123	8.6	9.1
124	8.6	9.1
125	8.6	9.0

126	8.6	9.0
127	8.6	9.1
128	8.6	9.1
129	12.3	12.7
130	3.2	4.1

131	8.7	10.1
132	12.5	13.9
133	3.2	5.7
134	8.8	11.4
135	12.7	15.0

136	3.2	7.2
137	8.9	15.9
138	3.2	8.2
139	3.2	16.7
140	3.2	17.1

141	3.2	17.5
142	3.2	18.0

143	3.2	18.4
144	3.2	18.7
145	3.2	18.4
146	3.2	17.7
147	3.2	16.9
148	3.2	16.0
149	3.3	14.8
150	3.3	14.8
151	3.3	14.9
152	3.3	15.1
153	3.3	15.2
154	3.3	15.3
155	3.3	15.4
156	3.3	15.6
157	3.3	15.7
158	3.3	15.7
159	3.2	11.6
160	3.2	11.7
161	3.2	11.8
162	3.2	12.0
163	3.2	12.1
164	3.2	12.2
165	9.1	12.4
166	4.0	4.5
167	9.0	9.1

168	12.2	12.6
169	8.9	9.3
170	4.0	4.5
171	9.0	9.5
172	3.9	4.4
173	9.2	9.8
174	3.9	4.4
175	9.3	10.0
176	3.8	4.4
177	9.5	10.2
178	3.8	4.4
179	9.6	10.3
180	3.7	4.4
181	9.6	10.3
182	3.7	5.0
183	9.4	10.2
184	3.6	6.3
185	9.1	10.2
186	3.7	10.2
187	3.8	10.2
188	3.9	10.1
189	4.0	10.1
190	4.0	10.1
191	4.1	10.1
192	4.2	10.0

193	4.3	10.0
194	4.4	10.0
195	4.4	10.0

- -

196	4.5	9.9
197	4.6	9.9
198	4.7	9.9
199	4.8	9.8
200	4.9	9.8

- -

201	4.9	9.8
202	5.0	9.7
203	5.1	9.7
204	5.2	9.6
205	5.3	9.5

- -

206	5.4	9.5
207	5.4	9.4
208	5.5	9.3
209	5.6	8.3
210	5.7	7.6

- -

211	5.8	6.9

Now that you finished marking- HAVE FUN FOLDING for a Harry Potter Fan!

Remember! When left or right folded paper is too long to lay flat because it extends beyond the book spine use scissors. Simply trim the excess in a straight line from page edge toward book spine and gently tear off the excess.

MyChicArt Book Folding Pattern for **Cat Woman Mask 190 Folds**
==
Instructions:
These measurements describe where to mark and fold the pages of your 20cm or longer book with at least 380-page numbers. All measurements are given in cm. The first number indicates the sheet number (2-page numbers equals one sheet, the second tells you where (measured with a metric ruler placed at the left edge of the page at the '0' mark) to mark and then fold the left corner down at a 90-degree angle; the third number tells you where to mark and then fold the right corner down at a 90-degree angle.

Sheet	Left Fold	Right Fold
1	9.8	11.3
2	9.5	11.6
3	9.3	11.9
4	9.1	12.1
5	8.9	12.3
6	8.8	12.4
7	8.6	12.6
8	8.4	12.7
9	8.3	12.8
10	8.2	12.9
11	8.1	13.0
12	7.9	13.1
13	7.8	13.2
14	7.5	13.3
15	6.8	13.4

16	6.4	13.5
17	6.0	13.6
18	5.7	13.7
19	5.5	13.7
20	5.2	13.8
21	5.0	13.9
22	4.8	13.9
23	4.6	14.0
24	4.4	14.1
25	4.2	14.1
26	4.0	14.2
27	3.9	14.2
28	3.7	14.3
29	3.6	14.3
30	3.4	14.4
31	3.3	14.4
32	3.2	14.5
33	10.8	14.5
34	3.1	10.3
35	11.0	14.6
36	3.3	10.2
37	11.3	14.7
38	3.5	10.1

39	11.4	14.8
40	3.7	10.0
41	11.6	14.9
42	3.9	9.9
43	11.7	15.0
44	4.1	9.9
45	11.8	15.0
46	4.3	9.8
47	11.9	15.1
48	4.6	9.8
49	11.9	15.2
50	4.8	9.8
51	12.0	15.2
52	5.2	9.8
53	12.0	15.3
54	5.5	9.8
55	12.0	15.3
56	5.8	9.8
57	12.0	15.3
58	6.2	9.9
59	12.0	15.4
60	6.3	9.9
61	12.0	15.4

62	6.3	10.0
63	12.0	15.5
64	6.2	10.0
65	12.0	15.5

66	6.1	10.1
67	11.9	15.6
68	6.0	10.2
69	11.9	15.6
70	6.0	10.3

71	11.8	15.7
72	5.9	10.5
73	11.7	15.7
74	5.9	10.7
75	11.6	15.7

76	5.8	10.9
77	11.4	15.8
78	5.8	15.8
79	5.8	15.8
80	5.8	15.8

81	5.7	15.8
82	5.7	15.8
83	5.7	15.9
84	5.7	15.9
85	5.7	15.9

86	5.7	15.9
87	5.7	15.9
88	5.7	15.9
89	5.7	15.9
90	5.7	15.9
91	5.7	15.9
92	5.6	15.9
93	5.6	15.9
94	5.6	15.9
95	5.6	15.9
96	5.6	15.9
97	5.6	15.9
98	5.6	15.9
99	5.6	15.9
100	5.6	15.9
101	5.6	15.9
102	5.6	15.9
103	5.7	15.9
104	5.7	15.9
105	5.7	15.9
106	5.7	15.9
107	5.7	15.9
108	5.7	15.9

109	5.7	15.8
110	5.7	15.8

111	5.7	15.8
112	5.8	15.8
113	5.8	15.8
114	5.8	15.8
115	5.8	15.8

116	5.8	15.8
117	11.5	15.7
118	5.9	10.9
119	11.6	15.7
120	5.9	10.7

121	11.7	15.7
122	6.0	10.5
123	11.8	15.6
124	6.0	10.3
125	11.9	15.6

126	6.1	10.2
127	12.0	15.5
128	6.2	10.2
129	12.0	15.5
130	6.2	10.1

131	12.0	15.4

132	6.3	10.0
133	12.0	15.4
134	6.3	9.9
135	12.0	15.3

136	6.1	9.9
137	12.0	15.3
138	5.9	9.8
139	12.0	15.3
140	5.6	9.8

141	12.0	15.2
142	5.3	9.8
143	11.9	15.1
144	5.0	9.8
145	11.9	15.1

146	4.7	9.8
147	11.8	15.0
148	4.4	9.9
149	11.7	15.0
150	4.2	9.9

151	11.6	14.9
152	4.0	9.9
153	11.5	14.8
154	3.8	10.0
155	11.3	14.8

----	----	----
156	3.6	10.1
157	11.1	14.7
158	3.5	10.2
159	10.9	14.6
160	3.3	10.3
----	----	----
161	3.4	14.5
162	3.5	14.4
163	3.6	14.4
164	3.7	14.3
165	3.8	14.3
----	----	----
166	4.0	14.2
167	4.1	14.2
168	4.3	14.1
169	4.5	14.0
170	4.7	14.0
----	----	----
171	4.9	13.9
172	5.1	13.8
173	5.3	13.8
174	5.5	13.7
175	5.7	13.6
----	----	----
176	6.0	13.5
177	6.3	13.4
178	6.7	13.3

179	7.3	13.2
180	8.1	13.1
-----	-----	-----
181	8.3	13.0
182	8.4	12.9
183	8.6	12.8
184	8.7	12.6
185	8.9	12.5
-----	-----	-----
186	9.0	12.3
187	9.2	12.2
188	9.4	11.9
189	9.7	11.7
190	10.0	11.3

Now that you have marked all the pages, **Have Fun Folding for a cat lover or Cat Woman fan!**

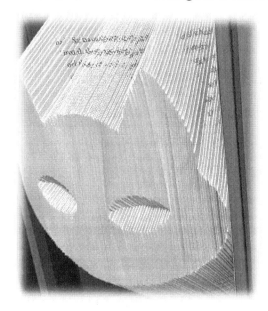

MyChicArt Book Folding Pattern for **Anchor 164 Folds**

===

Instructions:

These measurements describe where to mark and fold the pages of your 22cm or longer book with at least 328-page numbers. All measurements are given in cm. The first number indicates the sheet number (2-page numbers equals one sheet, the second tells you where (measured with a metric ruler placed at the left edge of the page at the '0' mark) to mark and then fold the left corner down at a 90-degree angle; the third number tells you where to mark and then fold the right corner down at a 90-degree angle.

Sheet	Left Fold	Right Fold
1	14.0	14.4
2	13.5	14.4
3	12.9	14.5
4	11.9	14.5
5	11.8	14.4
6	11.9	14.4
7	12.0	14.4
8	12.0	14.4
9	12.1	14.4
10	12.2	14.4
11	12.2	14.4
12	12.3	14.4
13	12.3	14.4
14	12.4	14.5
15	12.5	14.5
16	12.5	14.6
17	12.6	14.7
18	12.7	14.8

19	12.7	14.8
20	12.8	14.9

21	12.8	15.0
22	12.9	15.0
23	13.0	15.1
24	13.0	15.1
25	13.1	15.2

26	13.2	15.3
27	13.2	15.3
28	13.3	14.1
29	14.2	15.4
30	13.4	14.1

31	14.3	15.5
32	14.4	15.6
33	7.5	8.4
34	13.7	13.9
35	14.5	15.7

36	7.5	8.4
37	14.6	15.8
38	7.5	8.5
39	14.6	15.8
40	7.5	8.5

41	14.7	15.9
42	7.5	8.5
43	14.7	15.9

44	7.5	8.5
45	14.7	16.0

- -

46	7.5	8.5
47	14.8	16.1
48	7.5	8.5
49	14.8	16.1
50	7.5	8.5

- -

51	14.8	16.2
52	7.4	8.6
53	14.8	16.2
54	7.4	8.6
55	14.7	16.2

- -

56	7.4	8.6
57	14.7	16.3
58	7.4	8.6
59	14.7	16.3
60	5.2	6.2

- -

61	7.5	8.5
62	14.6	16.4
63	4.8	6.6
64	7.5	8.5
65	14.4	16.6

- -

66	4.6	6.8
67	7.5	8.5
68	14.1	16.7

69	6.0	6.9
70	7.5	8.5

71	13.5	16.8
72	4.3	5.1
73	5.7	16.9
74	4.3	4.9
75	5.4	17.1

76	4.3	4.9
77	5.3	17.2
78	4.2	4.8
79	5.3	17.4
80	4.2	4.8

81	5.2	17.6
82	4.2	4.8
83	5.2	17.7
84	4.2	4.8
85	5.2	17.5

86	4.2	4.8
87	5.3	17.3
88	4.2	4.8
89	5.4	17.2
90	4.3	4.9

91	5.5	17.0
92	4.3	5.0
93	6.0	7.0

94	7.5	8.5
95	13.8	16.8

96	4.5	5.4
97	7.5	8.5
98	14.2	16.6
99	4.6	6.8
100	7.5	8.5

101	14.4	16.5
102	4.8	6.6
103	7.5	8.5
104	14.6	16.4
105	5.2	6.2

106	7.4	8.6
107	14.7	16.3
108	7.4	8.6
109	14.7	16.3
110	7.4	8.6

111	14.8	16.2
112	7.4	8.6
113	14.8	16.2
114	7.4	8.6
115	14.8	16.1

116	7.5	8.5
117	14.8	16.1
118	7.5	8.5

119	14.8	16.0
120	7.5	8.5

121	14.7	16.0
122	7.5	8.5
123	14.7	15.9
124	7.5	8.5
125	14.7	15.9

126	7.5	8.5
127	14.6	15.8
128	7.5	8.5
129	7.5	8.4
130	13.7	13.9

131	14.5	15.6
132	7.5	8.4
133	13.5	14.0
134	13.5	14.0
135	14.3	15.5

136	13.3	14.1
137	14.2	15.4
138	13.2	15.3
139	13.2	15.3
140	13.1	15.2

141	13.0	15.1
142	13.0	15.1
143	12.9	15.0

144	12.8	15.0
145	12.8	14.9
- -		
146	12.7	14.8
147	12.7	14.8
148	12.6	14.7
149	12.5	14.6
150	12.5	14.5
- -		
151	12.4	14.5
152	12.3	14.4
153	12.3	14.4
154	12.2	14.4
155	12.2	14.4
- -		
156	12.1	14.4
157	12.0	14.4
158	12.0	14.4
159	11.9	14.4
160	11.8	14.4
- -		
161	11.9	14.5
162	12.9	14.5
163	13.5	14.4
164	14.0	14.4

Now that you have marked all the Sheets- **FOLDING for a Boating Fan!**

Remember! When left or right folded paper is too long to lay flat because it extends beyond the book spine use scissors. Simply trim the excess in a straight line from page edge toward book spine and gently tear off the excess.

===

Instructions:

These measurements describe where to fold the pages of your 20cm or larger book with at least 274 pages. All measurements are given in cm. The first number indicates the sheet number (2-page numbers equals one sheet), the second tells you where (measured with a cm ruler placed at the left edge of the page at the '0' mark) to mark and fold the left corner down at a 90-degree angle; the third tells you where to mark and fold the right corner down at a 90-degree angle.

Sheet	Left Fold	Right Fold
1	13.4	14.9
2	13.1	15.3
3	12.8	15.5
4	12.6	15.7
5	4.6	5.2
6	12.3	16.0
7	4.6	5.5
8	12.0	16.2
9	4.6	5.7
10	11.6	16.4
11	4.7	6.0
12	11.3	16.6
13	4.7	6.1
14	10.9	16.7
15	4.8	6.4
16	10.5	16.8

17	4.9	7.2
18	10.1	16.9
19	5.0	7.5
20	9.7	16.9

21	5.0	7.8
22	5.1	17.0
23	5.1	17.0
24	5.0	17.0
25	5.0	17.0

26	5.0	17.0
27	4.9	17.0
28	4.9	17.1
29	4.9	17.1
30	4.8	17.1

31	4.8	17.1
32	4.8	17.1
33	4.7	17.1
34	4.7	17.1
35	4.7	17.1

36	4.6	17.1
37	4.6	17.1
38	4.6	17.1
39	4.6	17.1
40	4.5	17.1

41	4.5	17.1

42	4.5	17.1
43	4.4	17.1
44	4.0	17.1
45	3.5	17.1
---	---	---
46	3.3	17.1
47	3.1	17.1
48	3.0	17.1
49	3.0	17.1
50	2.9	17.1
---	---	---
51	2.9	17.1
52	2.9	17.1
53	3.0	17.1
54	3.0	17.1
55	3.1	17.1
---	---	---
56	3.2	17.1
57	3.3	17.1
58	3.4	17.1
59	3.5	17.1
60	3.6	17.2
---	---	---
61	3.8	17.2
62	3.9	17.2
63	4.2	17.2
64	4.4	17.2
65	4.6	17.2
---	---	---
66	4.7	17.2

67	4.9	17.2
68	5.0	17.2
69	5.2	17.2
70	5.3	17.3

71	5.4	17.3
72	7.4	17.3
73	5.8	6.9
74	7.7	17.3
75	7.8	17.3

76	7.9	17.3
77	8.0	17.3
78	8.2	17.3
79	8.3	17.3
80	8.6	17.3

81	9.3	17.3
82	9.6	17.3
83	9.8	17.3
84	9.9	17.2
85	10.0	17.2

86	10.1	17.2
87	10.2	17.2
88	10.3	17.2
89	10.5	17.2
90	10.6	17.2

91	10.8	17.1

92	11.0	17.1
93	11.2	17.1
94	11.3	17.1
95	11.4	17.0

96	11.6	17.0
97	11.7	17.0
98	11.8	17.0
99	12.0	16.9
100	12.1	16.9

101	12.3	16.9
102	12.5	16.8
103	12.8	14.9
104	15.1	16.7
105	15.0	16.7

106	14.9	16.6
107	14.8	16.6
108	14.7	16.5
109	14.5	16.5
110	14.3	16.4

111	14.1	16.4
112	13.7	16.3
113	10.6	16.2
114	10.4	16.2
115	10.3	16.1

116	10.1	16.0

117	10.0	15.9
118	9.9	15.9
119	9.8	15.8
120	9.8	15.7

- -

121	9.7	15.5
122	9.6	15.4
123	9.6	15.2
124	9.5	15.1
125	9.4	11.1

- -

126	12.9	14.5
127	9.3	10.7
128	9.3	10.6
129	9.3	10.5
130	9.3	10.4

- -

131	9.2	10.3
132	9.2	10.2
133	9.3	10.2
134	9.3	10.1
135	9.3	10.0

- -

136	9.4	9.9
137	9.5	9.8

Now that you have marked all the Sheets- **HAVE FUN FOLDING!**

==

Instructions:

These measurements describe where to fold the pages of your 20cm or larger book with at least 230 pages. All measurements are given in cm. The first number indicates the sheet number (2-page numbers equals one sheet), the second tells you where (measured with a metric ruler placed at the left edge of the page at the '0' mark) to mark and fold the left corner down at a 90-degree angle, the third tells you where to mark and fold the right corner down at a 90-degree angle.

Sheet	Left Fold	Right Fold
1	9.6	10.2
2	9.4	10.5
3	9.2	10.7
4	9.1	10.8
5	9.1	10.9
6	9.0	11.0
7	9.0	11.1
8	8.9	11.1
9	8.9	11.2
10	8.9	11.2
11	8.9	11.2
12	8.9	11.3
13	8.9	11.3
14	8.9	11.3
15	8.9	11.3
16	9.0	11.3

17	9.0	11.3
18	12.5	13.3
19	9.1	11.3
20	12.0	13.6
21	9.2	11.2
22	11.7	13.8
23	9.4	11.1
24	11.5	13.9
25	11.4	14.0
26	7.9	8.9
27	9.9	10.8
28	11.1	14.0
29	7.5	9.4
30	10.9	14.1
31	7.4	9.5
32	10.8	14.1
33	7.3	9.6
34	10.6	14.1
35	7.2	9.7
36	10.5	14.1
37	7.2	9.8
38	10.4	14.1
39	7.2	9.8
40	10.3	14.0
41	7.2	9.8

42	10.2	14.0
43	7.2	9.8
44	10.1	13.9
45	7.3	9.8

46	10.0	13.9
47	7.4	9.7
48	10.0	13.8
49	7.5	9.6
50	9.9	13.8

51	7.7	9.5
52	9.9	13.7
53	7.9	9.3
54	9.8	13.7
55	8.3	9.0

56	9.8	13.8
57	9.8	13.8
58	9.8	13.8
59	9.8	13.8
60	9.8	13.8

61	8.5	9.3
62	9.9	13.9
63	8.1	9.5
64	9.9	13.9
65	7.9	9.7

66	10.0	14.0

67	7.7	9.8
68	10.1	14.0
69	7.6	9.9
70	10.2	14.0

71	7.5	9.9
72	10.3	14.0
73	7.4	9.9
74	10.4	14.1
75	7.3	9.9

76	10.6	14.0
77	7.3	9.9
78	10.7	14.0
79	7.3	9.9
80	10.9	14.0

81	7.3	9.8
82	11.1	13.9
83	7.4	9.7
84	10.5	10.7
85	11.4	13.8

86	7.5	9.6
87	10.0	11.2
88	11.7	13.6
89	7.8	9.3
90	9.7	11.4

91	12.2	13.3

92	12.5	13.0
93	9.5	11.5
94	9.5	11.5
95	9.4	11.5
-------	-------	-------
96	9.4	11.5
97	9.3	11.5
98	9.3	11.5
99	9.3	11.5
100	9.3	11.5
-------	-------	-------
101	9.3	11.5
102	9.2	11.5
103	9.2	11.5
104	9.2	11.5
105	9.3	11.5
-------	-------	-------
106	9.3	11.4
107	9.3	11.4
108	9.3	11.3
109	9.3	11.3
110	9.4	11.2
-------	-------	-------
111	9.4	11.1
112	9.5	11.0
113	9.6	10.9
114	9.7	10.7
115	10.0	10.4

Now that you have marked all the Sheets- **HAVE FUN FOLDING!**

MyChicArt Book Folding Pattern for **Butterfly 162 Folds**

==

Instructions:

These measurements describe where to mark and fold the pages of your 20cm or longer book with at least 324-page numbers. All measurements are given in cm. The first number indicates the sheet number (2-page numbers equals one sheet), the second tells you where (measured with a metric ruler placed at the left edge of the page at the '0' mark) to mark and then fold the left corner down at a 90-degree angle; the third number tells you where to mark and then fold the right corner down at a 90-degree angle.

Sheet	Left Fold	Right Fold
1	5.2	5.4
2	4.9	5.7
3	4.6	6.1
4	4.5	6.4
5	4.5	6.7
6	4.5	6.9
7	4.5	7.2
8	4.5	7.5
9	4.5	7.8
10	11.5	13.1
11	4.5	8.7
12	11.4	13.4
13	4.6	9.6
14	10.9	13.6
15	4.6	9.9
16	10.8	13.8

17	4.7	10.1
18	10.6	14.0
19	4.8	10.2
20	10.5	14.1
21	4.8	10.3
22	4.9	14.2
23	4.9	14.3
24	5.0	14.4
25	5.0	14.4
26	5.1	14.5
27	5.1	14.5
28	5.2	14.6
29	5.3	14.7
30	5.3	14.7
31	5.4	14.7
32	5.5	14.8
33	5.5	14.8
34	5.6	14.8
35	5.7	14.9
36	5.7	14.9
37	5.8	14.9
38	5.9	14.9
39	5.9	14.9
40	6.0	14.9
41	6.1	14.9

42	6.2	14.8
43	6.2	14.8
44	6.3	14.7
45	6.4	14.6
--------	--------	--------
46	6.5	14.5
47	6.5	14.4
48	6.6	14.3
49	6.7	14.3
50	6.8	14.2
--------	--------	--------
51	6.9	14.1
52	7.0	14.0
53	7.0	14.0
54	7.1	13.9
55	7.2	13.9
--------	--------	--------
56	7.3	13.8
57	7.4	13.8
58	7.5	13.7
59	7.6	13.7
60	7.7	13.6
--------	--------	--------
61	7.8	13.5
62	7.9	13.5
63	8.0	13.4
64	8.1	13.3
65	8.3	13.2
--------	--------	--------
66	8.4	13.1

67	8.7	13.0
68	8.8	12.9
69	9.0	12.9
70	9.1	13.3
71	9.1	13.8
72	9.2	13.7
73	9.3	13.6
74	9.3	13.3
75	9.0	12.7
76	8.9	12.6
77	8.9	12.5
78	8.9	12.6
79	8.9	12.9
80	9.6	13.2
81	9.2	9.3
82	9.6	13.7
83	9.5	13.9
84	9.5	14.0
85	9.4	14.2
86	9.3	14.3
87	9.2	14.5
88	9.2	14.6
89	9.1	14.7
90	9.0	14.8
91	9.0	14.9

92	8.9	15.0
93	8.8	15.1
94	8.8	15.2
95	8.7	15.2
96	8.7	15.3
97	8.6	15.3
98	8.6	15.4
99	8.5	15.4
100	8.4	15.4
101	8.4	15.5
102	8.3	15.5
103	8.3	15.5
104	8.2	15.6
105	8.2	15.6
106	8.1	15.6
107	8.1	15.6
108	8.0	15.6
109	8.0	15.7
110	8.0	15.7
111	7.9	15.7
112	7.9	15.7
113	7.8	15.7
114	7.8	15.7
115	7.8	15.7
116	7.7	15.7

117	7.7	15.7
118	7.7	15.7
119	7.7	15.7
120	7.6	15.7
121	7.6	15.6
122	7.6	15.6
123	7.6	15.5
124	7.5	15.5
125	7.5	15.4
126	7.5	15.3
127	7.5	15.2
128	7.5	15.1
129	7.4	15.0
130	12.3	14.9
131	7.4	12.2
132	12.5	14.6
133	7.4	12.1
134	12.8	14.2
135	7.3	12.1
136	7.3	12.0
137	7.3	11.9
138	7.3	11.9
139	7.3	11.8
140	7.3	11.7
141	7.3	11.6

142	7.2	11.4
143	7.2	11.0
144	7.2	10.6
145	7.2	10.4
- - - - - - - - - - - - - - -		
146	7.2	10.2
147	7.2	10.1
148	7.2	9.9
149	7.2	9.8
150	7.2	9.7
- - - - - - - - - - - - - - -		
151	7.2	9.5
152	7.2	9.4
153	7.2	9.3
154	7.2	9.2
155	7.2	9.0
- - - - - - - - - - - - - - -		
156	7.2	8.9
157	7.2	8.7
158	7.2	8.6
159	7.2	8.4
160	7.2	8.2
- - - - - - - - - - - - - - -		
161	7.2	7.9
162	7.3	7.5

Now that you finished marking- FOLD and Finish!

Remember! When left or right folded paper is too long to lay flat because it extends beyond the book spine use scissors. Simply trim the excess in a straight line from page edge toward book spine and gently tear off the excess.

Book Folding Questions Answered

View additional FAQ & Ask your own Questions at www.mychicart.com

How long will it take to complete a book?

The time is takes to complete a folded book project varies depending on the pattern and the folder! Most folded books using MyChicArt Patterns can be marked and folded in 2-6 hours. A good way to estimate time needed is to calculate 2 hours for every 100 folds. For example, if a Pattern specifies 193 Folds, assume 4 hours to complete. Add any time to 'finish' or decorate the book (i.e., ribbon, embellishments) to your estimate.

Is this a measure and fold or is there cutting involved?

MyChicArt Patterns designed for beginners are measure, mark, fold patterns. There are generally 2 marks, and 2 folds per page (or sheet of paper.) Cutting will only occur when both marks on the same sheet are very high or very low. In these instances, one horizontal cut may be necessary to ensure the sheet does not extend beyond the book spine when folded.

Can I open the book wider to display it, or will it ruin it?

You can open the book as wide as you prefer to display it; this will not affect the folded art at all! Some prefer to display as a standalone, others wedge the book between other books or objects for a more compressed look. If over time the design spreads too wide for your taste simply close the book, lay it on it's side, and stack a couple of heavy books on it for a day.

You say to use a 'gently read' book. Where do I find this?

Used hardcover books can be found at book sales in libraries, school fairs, tag sales, online at eBay or Amazon, and on your own bookshelf! "Gently Read" simply means a used book in very good to like new condition. Remove the dust jacket and inspect the cover. It should be clean and free from dents. Look for a book with a tight binding. When the book is closed, the page edges should be free from pencil, marker, or dirt. Find a cover color to fit your décor. Or find a book title that matches the fold, or the recipient when folding for a gift.

What is the best way to tie back my extra pages with ribbon?

The extra pages in front of and immediately following your folded art design can be bound using any type of ribbon and double-sided tape. Wrap the ribbon around the unused pages and the book cover on each side to measure the amount needed. Add approximately 2 extra inches to the length and cut. Add 1-2 inches of tape on the very end. Wrap the ribbon around the book cover and secure the opposite end over the tape in a tight fit. The taped part can be hidden by moving the edge behind your first fold.

Book Folding Calculation Worksheet		Example	Your Calculation
The last even numbered page in your book		320	
Divide by 2 to get the total foldable **sheets** of paper in your chosen book.	/2	160	
Subtract **Folds** required indicated at top of every MyChicArt Pattern.	-	99	
Your starting page number* *This number is typically an odd number; if it is an even number simply add 1 and this will be the first page you mark.		61	
NOTES:			

Book Folding Calculation Worksheet		Example	Your Calculation
The last even numbered page in your book		320	
Divide by 2 to get the total foldable **sheets** of paper in your chosen book.	/2	160	
Subtract **Folds** required indicated at top of every MyChicArt Pattern.	-	99	
Your starting page number* *This number is typically an odd number; if it is an even number simply add 1 and this will be the first page you mark.		61	
NOTES:			

Book Folding Calculation Worksheet		Example	Your Calculation
The last even numbered <u>page</u> in your book		320	
Divide by 2 to get the total foldable **sheets** of paper in your chosen book.	/2	160	
Subtract **Folds** required indicated at top of every MyChicArt Pattern.	-	99	
Your starting page number* *This number is typically an odd number; if it is an even number simply add 1 and this will be the first page you mark.		61	
NOTES:			

Book Folding Calculation Worksheet		Example	Your Calculation
The last even numbered <u>page</u> in your book		320	
Divide by 2 to get the total foldable **sheets** of paper in your chosen book.	/2	160	
Subtract **Folds** required indicated at top of every MyChicArt Pattern.	-	99	
Your starting page number* *This number is typically an odd number; if it's an even number simply add 1 and this will be the first page you mark.		61	
NOTES:			

My Book Folding Notes...

Made in the USA
Columbia, SC
19 December 2024

49935180R00098